Song After All

The letters of Reginald Shepherd and Alan Contreras, 2007-2008

including related essays and commentary

with **Fernando Pessoa's** *Antinous*

Foreword and Additional Essays
by
Robert Philen

Alan Contreras, Editor

CraneDance
2013

ISBN 978-0-9893848-3-4

CRANEDANCE PUBLICATIONS
PO BOX 50535, Eugene, OR 97405
541-345-3974

Song After All

To the memory of my unmet friend Reginald

Contents

Acknowledgements and Derivations... ii

Foreword *Robert Philen* iii

Introduction 1

The correspondence.. 11

Incorporated essays, blog posts and related commentary:

AC: I'm an Expert, or how I lenskafied myself................................... 67
AC: Reginald Shepherd's *Orpheus in the Bronx* 163
AC: The Ins and Outs of Online Dating... 91
AC: Three Short Reviews.. 20
AC: Alex Ross's *The Rest is Noise*... 106
AC: Hivewriting.. 122
AC: Music for the Ages 95
AC: Ned Rorem and the Future of American Song 33
AC: The Risk of Reading 145
Evan Eisenberg: Poetic License Exam 78
Fernando Pessoa: *Antinous* 171
RP Reading, Looking, Listening.. 17
RP Stravinsky's Rite of Spring and the Experience of Art
     (Musical and Visual).. 14
RP The Experience of Live Music 29
RS: Ann Lauterbach on Schools, Movements, and Poetic Identities....... 62
RS: Gay Male Poetry Post Identity Politics, Part Two 134
RS: On George Barker.. 42
RS: Reflections on Poetry and Disaster 56
RS: Working Class Hero... 84

Index... 183

i

Acknowledgements and Derivations

E-mails and blog posts by Reginald Shepherd are reproduced here courtesy Robert Philen, Shepherd's literary executor.

Writing by Reginald Shepherd (from his blog)

"On George Barker" appeared May 13, 2007.
"Reflections on Poetry and Disaster" appeared July 2, 2007.
"Ann Lauterbach on Schools, Movements, and Poetic Identities" appeared July 8, 2007.
"Working Class Hero" appeared August 25, 2007.
"Gay Male Poetry Post Identity Politics, Part Two" appeared February 8, 2008.

Writing by Robert Philen (from his blog)

"Stravinsky's Rite of Spring and the Experience of Art (Musical and Visual)" appeared April 16, 2007.
"Reading, Looking, Listening" appeared April 25, 2007.
"The Experience of Live Music" appeared June 19, 2007.

Writing by Alan Contreras (from the blog *The Oregon Review* and other publications)

Part of the introduction is from "Honoring a Lost Poetic Voice" and appeared in *Inside Higher Education* on October 16, 2008.
"Alex Ross's *The Rest is Noise*" appeared on *The Oregon Review* in December, 2007.
"Music for the Ages" appeared on *The Oregon Review* in November, 2007.
"The Ins and Outs of Online Dating" appeared on *The Oregon Review* November 3, 2007.
"Hivewriting" appeared as "The Moated Castles of Today's Poetry" on *The Oregon Review* on February 2, 2008.
"Ned Rorem and American Song" appeared on *The Oregon Review* on July 28, 2007.
"The Risk of Reading" appeared on *The Oregon Review* on July 30, 2007.
"Reginald Shepherd's *Orpheus in the Bronx*" appeared on *The Oregon Review* June 8, 2008.

"Antinous" by Fernando Pessoa was written in English in Portugal in 1918 and is in the public domain, though it is rarely seen.

Foreword

People, especially in the often over-specialized world of academe, sometimes think I'm scattered in my thinking and interests. I've written on topics of race and ethnicity; health, disease, and culture; gender and sexuality; music – from bebop to boy bands; Lévi-Straussean structuralism; alcohol; and poetry. I shared with Reginald Shepherd during our time together a broad ranging and voracious appetite for discussion and consideration of everything – and why shouldn't we be interested in everything. Our conversations were free ranging, delving into our respective professional fields – Poetry, Literature, and English for his part, Anthropology for mine – but also circumambulating regularly through the fields of music, paleontology, politics, history, birds, and food. This freewheeling attitude toward topics of thought readily fit both our temperaments and perhaps our choice of professional fields – where in both cases we had gravitated toward fields where specialization is certainly possible but by no means necessary, and where a generalizing attitude can serve one well.

But neither Reginald nor I were/are actually scattered in our thinking. Despite interest in a wide variety of topics, we both shared a synthetic approach, attempting to draw connections between seemingly disparate things. This came across in Shepherd's conversations with others, here with his correspondence, or in his poetry – for example in his usage of Classical allusions and imagery alongside contemporary realities, including realities of gay and/or black experience.

There were also shared themes that oriented our coupled thinking on the wide variety of topics we set our minds to, including the relationship between discourse and practice. In relation to poetry and writing in general, we shared an interest in the relationship between writing, the world, and action in the world. Some of Shepherd's critics frankly don't get his frequent use of Classical imagery – Why did he need the mythology to express contemporary gay and/or black experience? Leaving aside for the moment his aversion to seeing poetry as expression, seeing it rather as the production of an enduring aesthetic object with its own existence, it's true that Classical allusion isn't needed to express some version of black or gay experience, but to express what he wanted, it was, and it was no less "black" or "gay" for it.

In his autobiographical essays, Shepherd wrote about Modernist poetry and mythology and the Classical World (through the lens of Edith Hamilton, Robert Graves, Bulfinch and others) as things that provided for him, a young gay, black man growing up in poverty in the Bronx, what Adorno discussed as the alienation of one's alienation – providing him with a view, really his only view, of how things could be different. In other words, it was partly through Modernist poetry and Classical mythology that Reginald Shepherd was able to become a self-actualized adult black, gay man. So, how could these things not be part of his expressions of gayness and blackness?

Shepherd really had a nuanced, yet still straightforward stance on the relationship between poetry/writing, social position, and praxis. His view in a nutshell was that poetry or other art is inevitably shaped by the social circumstances surrounding its production, but that art is never wholly determined by those social surroundings, nor its meaning wholly reduced to them.

As I write this, I have recently been reading Enrique Krauze's book *The Redeemers*, about key intellectuals and artists in recent Latin American history. I am struck by the degree to which José Carlos Mariátegui stands as a kindred Latin American spirit with Reginald. The early 20th Century Peruvian Marxist philosopher and writer shared with Shepherd an outsider's view of the workings of power, and an interest in social justice, but also an absolute emphasis on aesthetic quality in and of itself and an emphasis on individual possibility. For both this entailed an ability to respect the work even of one's nemeses.

One thing we see clearly in Shepherd's correspondences is the respect he often held for works of individuals he sometimes personally despised. Shepherd's ability to separate feelings about the person and the person's work is all too rare nowadays. This ability on his part is no doubt linked to his cultivation of an aesthetic position emphasizing the autonomy of both the artist and the work of art, while the rarity of this skill is no doubt linked to the widespread tendency to reduce art to personal expression or symptom of the artist's biography.

We see all of these qualities and positions playing out in this series of Shepherd's correspondences with Alan Contreras. But also some of the pleasures and pains involved in staking out an aesthetic space and the social interchanges involved in the production of ideas. We see the creative process unfolding in the medium of these letters. Which is not to imply that the ideas are half-baked here. Reginald was always meticulous and substantive in his words in even the most trifling of conversations, though also witty, passionate, occasionally biting, ordinarily loving.

Robert Philen
Pensacola, Florida
January, 2013

Introduction

In one of his short notes, Albert Camus speculates on a dinner conversation with André Gide in which Gide gives this response to young writers who ask if they should continue: "What? You can keep yourself from writing and you hesitate to do so?"[1] Reginald Shepherd was fortunately not subject to any desire to stop writing; indeed quite the opposite. For that we can all be grateful.

This collection is intended to introduce the reader to its writers, particularly the late Reginald Shepherd, whose six books of poetry, two collections of critical comment and several edited collections form a significant component of modern American poetic literature. Reginald's death from cancer at the age of 45 affected me personally, although I never met him. We corresponded by e-mail for 17 months and I donated the funds to bring him to speak and read at the University of Oregon. He died before he could come, but those funds and additional donations have been used to establish a student poetry prize in his name and memory at Oregon. Royalties from this book will be used to maintain that prize fund.

How best can we honor a poet by recognizing the work of another poet, and how can that unique gift, a poet's voice, be properly set forth for the view of history, other than through the poems? It is easy enough to honor an historian with a prize celebrating new work in that field, or a particle physicist by establishing the Quark Jockey of the Year or some similar clearly related award. But how should we set the criteria for a prize honoring the life and work of a lost poet? Unless that poet wrote about one thing or only in a single form, the life, the work and even to some extent the "voice" are quite varied. Reginald's interests were broad; his work was eclectic in subject if less so in voice. The prize is therefore necessarily a work in progress, as are all writers.

I have to offer at least some minimal descriptions. Reginald's work—though we never met he always signed with his first name—was certainly borne aloft on the great wings of

---

[1] Albert Camus, *Notebooks 1942-1951*, p. 201. Trans. Justin O'Brien. Paragon (1991).

candor, so we can't have any prize winners who waffle, fudge or hide the toys. Nor can we have mere diction-divers who, upon surfacing, scatter words here and there to see what happens. One of Reginald's mentors, the great science-fiction writer and essayist Samuel R. Delany, would eat us alive—dead or not—if we honored something sloppy.

I once described Reginald's work in a review as having "intense volcanic roiling," but I'm not sure that helps guide a student writer. There are similarities between describing poetry and describing wine: the pyramid of meaning starts with some clarity but rapidly widens into a turbid swirl of ungraspable sparkles.

We should certainly honor his breadth of emotion, which in turn reflected the life of a black gay man growing up in the Bronx and eventually passing through the University of Iowa and Cornell. Yes, but emotion is a genus, not a species. We all see and feel differently: Stephen Maturin reminds us that "the kinds of happiness are not to be compared."[2] Poetic emotion can appear in the urbane scrollwork of J. D. McClatchy, the high church pointillism of Carl Phillips, the mythic immersions of Cameron La Follette, the whisper-forest of W. S. Merwin. They are utterly different and all among my favorite poets.

It is sometimes easier to describe what a poet didn't do and didn't like rather than to classify his work into a poetic taxonomy. There were no pallid stones in Reginald's lapidarium, he had no time for the poetry of pathological personalism, he recognized that below a certain point economy of expression becomes chastity of imagination, he had no allergy to facts and he didn't geld any lilies merely because critics preferred parsnips—let the lilies show their stuff.

Reginald was a remarkable correspondent. He is the only person with whom I intentionally saved an entire e-correspondence and those 120 messages, treated as letters, constitute the bulk of this book, as the best memorial I can offer in addition to the prize. Perhaps my retention of those messages was a premonition that it would end too soon.

---

[2] Patrick O'Brian places this perfect statement on the tongue of Maturin in the novel *The Nutmeg of Consolation*, p. 258.

2

One example of how multiple subjects could gracefully occupy a small space in his writing is this, a single message on November 19, 2007:

"If I ever find out what "emo" means, I will let you know. I did a reading at Columbia University week before last and asked some of the students there, but didn't get a clear answer. I think it's music by "sensitive" but definitely straight boys who play guitar and may or may not wear eyeliner. Fall Out Boy seems to have something to do with it.

I too came across Aqualung by accident, having seen "Pressure Suit" (from his second U.S. album) on TV and then backtracked to his first U.S. album (which is a compilation of two UK albums, which I might try to track down). I adore "Strange and Beautiful" and also "Falling Out of Love," as well as "Good Times Gonna Come" and "Another Little Hole."

That's a good point about my colonization being the problem to begin with. Damned imperialist cancer! And now I'm partially decolonized. Does that mean I'm a dominion or a commonwealth or something, like Puerto Rico?"

Ultimately, his published work demonstrated with sometimes painful clarity the great canyon between those who play the instrument and those who play the music. Many poets never cross it. Reginald Shepherd played the music as well as anyone, and that's what we'd like the prize winners to do as well.

Reginald has now gone on the long and terrible way, to borrow an ancient phrase used in Theodore Roethke's *The Marrow*, and we who remain can honor him best by never forgetting what he really stood for: no halfway house for the intellect, no auto-referential academic priapism. The best, always, or why bother?

In *Orpheus in the Bronx*[3] he noted that there is a mainstream of American poetry, "broad, sluggish and muddy" that offers

---

[3] *Orpheus in the Bronx*, 2007. Michigan.

"convenient epiphanies in prosaic anecdotes not interesting or shapely enough to be short stories." His own work, issued to date in six collections,[4] is never sluggish or muddy, and glutinous turbidity will not be allowed of the prize winners. Instead we will require purity, light, joy and truth of the kind that he displayed in one of his masterpieces, "You, Therefore," included in his 2007 collection *Fata Morgana* and dedicated to his partner, Robert Philen, which begins:

> You are like me, you will die, too, but not today:
> you, incommensurate, therefore the hours shine...

and ends:

> ... home is nowhere, therefore you,
> a kind of dwell and welcome, song after all,
> and free of any eden we can name.

Let us recall Elliott Coues's definition of genius as "that union of passion and patience which bears fruit unknown to passion alone; to patience alone impossible."[5] Reginald's passionate genius outraced his patience as his illness progressed, and we are fortunate in that at least one posthumous poetry collection has appeared, along with the posthumously published essays in *A Martian Muse*.[6]

In the final essay in *Orpheus*, he answered the question "Why I Write" by saying "I write because I want to live forever," a straightforward and heartfelt restatement of Gide's desire to "have something secure against death."[7] The blooms of his genius are exsanguinated, but we can honor their living colors

---

[4] *Some are Drowning*, 1994; *Angel, Interrupted*, 1996; *Wrong*, 1999; *Otherhood*, 2003; *Fata Morgana*, 2007; *Red Clay Weather*, 2011; all from Pittsburgh.

[5] Elliott Coues, in *Behind the Veil* (1880), cited in *Elliott Coues: Naturalist and Frontier Historian*, p. 429. Paul R. Cutright and Michael J. Brodhead, 1981. Illinois.

[6] *A Martian Muse*, 2010. Michigan.

[7] The full statement, from Vol. 2 of the *Journals of André Gide*, Justin O'Brien, trans. (1948), p. 306 is "The reasons that impel me to write are multiple, and the most important ones, it seems to me, are the most secret. Perhaps this one above all: to have something secure against death—and this is what makes me, in my writings, seek among all other qualities those upon which time has the least grasp and by which they escape all passing fads."

4

forever with as many Reginald Shepherd Prizes and other joys as those of us who knew him can imagine. This collection is intended to be part of that picture.

Phil Ochs wrote in his spectacular song-poem "Crucifixion"[8] that "success is an enemy to the losers of the day." Reginald received his share of criticism from miscellaneous losers. That his name will outlast theirs becomes more evident with each passing season.

Letters in the modern world

This exchange of e-mail correspondence is called "letters" and it is, to a significant extent, the equivalent of letters formerly sent between literary friends and writers. There are many examples of such published letters and they sometimes vary greatly in tone and substance, even when originating from one writer, depending on to whom the letters were sent.

For example, the correspondence of André Gide and Paul Valéry[9] focused primarily on their lives as writers, travels and relationships with others, while Czeslaw Milosz and Thomas Merton[10] wrote about a wider variety of subjects, sometimes their writing but also the state of the world and what other authors had done. Merton, however, wrote with a much different tone and focus to his college friend, the writer Robert Lax, with whom he often exchanged casual and lighthearted

---

[8] I recommend Glenn Yarbrough's performance of "Crucifixion" because the best Phil Ochs performance (a live one) is hard to find and is, as of this writing, not available online. Another excellent version is by Jim and Jean, available online. The original studio recording by Ochs features shockingly ill-conceived orchestration.

[9] *Self-Portraits: The Gide-Valéry Letters, 1890-1942*. Ed. Robert Mallett, abridged and translated by June Guicharnaud, 1966 (Chicago). To give an idea of the changing role of letters as a part of daily life for literary people, consider that full-length collections have been published not only of Gide-Valéry, but of Gide-Edmund Gosse, Gide-Dorothy Bussy, Gide-Paul Claudel, Gide-Arnold Bennett and something similar for Gide-Oscar Wilde. To be sure, Gide was an extraordinarily productive writer who lived to write, but one cannot imagine anything remotely close to his output of letters today.

[10] *Striving Towards Being: the Letters of Thomas Merton and Czeslaw Milosz*, ed. Robert Faggen, 1996. Farrar Straus Giroux.

chatter about sex and what food he was eating, although to be sure they also discussed literature.[11]

The unique loveliness of work that can be found solely in collected letters is illustrated by this excerpt from the Gide-Valéry correspondence:

> "At sixteen, we would have been able to wander over the roads together, we would have had the sea at our right, the lonely East at our left, and before us, at a great distance, some venturesome inn in which to try our luck at satisfying all those hungers.

> "At night we would have pressed our faces to the windows, to see families preparing for happiness; and we would have gone down the chimney into rooms that otherwise were too calm, and we would have frightened the people who were about to fall asleep.

> "In the morning, before dawn, we would have had a swim and we would not have had headaches."

André Gide to Paul Valéry, December 15, 1895.

If you read the letters of Federico Garcia Lorca[12] you will find everything from nearly complete poetic drafts to his unique wiry drawings to self-flagellation over the perceived failure of a particular work. John Jay Chapman wrote to an extraordinary range of people about politics, literature, religion, philosophy and the processes of daily life, though his flagellation was mainly directed at others.[13]

In the absence of significant assemblages of hard copy letters between writers and other figures in today's world, e-mail is in fact a significant source of information about the life and work of writers, artists and others working in the fine arts and other fields. It is, however, difficult to collect in an orderly way,

---

[11] *When Prophecy Still Had a Voice: the Letters of Thomas Merton and Robert Lax.* Arthur Biddle, ed., 2001. Univ. Kentucky Press.

[12] *Federico Garcia Lorca, Selected Letters.* David Gershator, ed. and translator, 1983. New Directions.

[13] *John Jay Chapman and his Letters.* M. A. DeWolfe Howe, ed., 1937. Houghton Mifflin.

6

often mixed with a spray of technical chatter between mechanical devices and rarely thought of the way letters are – or were, there being very few letters today in the usual sense that the word has been used historically.

Ned Rorem discussed the nature of this transition in the introductory material to his own recent collection of letters.[14] He also noted that it is very difficult to obtain permission to include all of the responses to his own letters, so only his were included in the collection. This does provide a legitimate historical archive, akin to that provided for some American historical figures in the "Library of America" series, but it does not offer the sense of interaction that can be had from seeing both sides of a correspondence. James Merrill wrote that he enjoyed setting words spinning off each other like billiard balls,[15] and that is partly lost in a one-sided collection. That is why I have tried to include as much of the back-and-forth of our conversation as possible. I am grateful to Shepherd's partner and literary executor Robert Philen for his willingness to support this approach to sharing Shepherd's legacy.

The content of this volume

This book consists in significant part of e-mail messages exchanged between me and Reginald from April 2007 until his death in September, 2008. Within a few months of the beginning of our exchange, Shepherd began having medical problems, as I attempted to schedule him for a reading at the University of Oregon. These issues continued off and on for the 17 months of our correspondence, though he maintained a remarkable commitment to communication until a few weeks before his death, by which time he "belonged to this world only by courtesy," as Lord Moran put it.[16]

A few minor typos have been corrected and a small number of words have been added in brackets where the writer obviously

---

[14] Ned Rorem, *Wings of Friendship, Selected Letters, 1944-2003*, 2005. Shoemaker-Hoard.

[15] James Merrill, in an interview with John Boatwright and Enrique Ucelay DaCal, in J. D. McClatchy and Stephen Yenser, eds., *Collected Prose: James Merrill*, p. 71, 2004. Knopf.

[16] Lord Moran (Charles McMoran Wilson, 1st Baron Moran of Manton), *The Anatomy of Courage*, p. 154, 2007 (1945). Constable & Robinson.

intended them to be. In a couple of cases, private addresses have been deleted. The names of books and journals have been standardized, italicized and footnoted for the reader's convenience. A very small number of messages appear to have been lost and those places are marked when they are clear.

In a few cases a portion of the "conversation" moved briefly either to my blog or his, or to a discussion of some other item posted online, often my essays in the higher education media or Robert's blog. In most cases those "external" texts have been included where they naturally fall in chronological sequence, in order that the correspondence make more sense to a reader and that related material reside in one place rather than be scattered all over the Internet and therefore subject to change or deletion. The notion that electronic venues are somehow more "permanent" than traditional print books is, of course, nonsense.

I have no illusions that my own views and opinions expressed in this correspondence have a value or interest in the literary world equal to his. I am a well-known author of nature books and an expert on arcane aspects of higher education law, but I do not usually operate in the literary arena that was Reginald's. I publish the full correspondence that I kept in order to honor his memory and, in a way, to consummate our unique friendship.

The exchange set forth here consists of 120 messages, some rather long and a few quite short. They cover a variety of subjects, but the bulk include Reginald's thoughts (and sometimes mine) regarding poetry, music, occasionally other branches of literature and the fine arts, the place of gay people in society, the mechanics of writing and of poetry readings, his upcoming books, relationships and domestic life.

The essays and blog posts

Robert and I decided that there is some value to readers in my including here the blog posts, essays and the like on the subjects that Reginald and I discussed, mostly literature and music. Most of these are referred to directly in the correspondence, a few are merely ancillary stage-setting.

Much of his output on these subjects has been published elsewhere; some of mine has not, as I have written primarily in the field of higher education and natural history. Reginald, although his surviving partner Robert is a birder and naturalist, once told me that for him, "a little nature goes a long way." He has that in common with our more urban poets: J. D. McClatchy, another of my favorite poets, considers the natural world "uncongenial" as a poetic topic. I hope that readers will indulge me in these inclusions and view them as, in effect, minor planets in Copernican swirl around the more important conversation, providing occasional anchor points in space.

An essay is necessarily a risk. It involves extending the self into written form. Its greatest practitioners, Michel de Montaigne, Albert Camus, Gore Vidal, Paul Valéry, Camille Paglia, John Jay Chapman, Ralph Waldo Emerson, C.E.S. Wood, André Gide and others, all took risks, albeit of different kinds. At its best, the essay form helps us revisit, review and rethink our world. Many of Reginald's do this. I hope that a few of mine and Robert's accomplish this as well.

The problem of getting outside oneself in some way in order to obtain the panoramic view necessary to determine what questions should be asked and their answers attempted is an underrated problem in all fields. It is at least partly a matter of training, in the inward sense of the term that is more common in, say, martial arts than in electronics. Our society does not encourage careful, evaluative observation of much of anything, let alone the self. The British philosopher Michael Oakeshott wrote that

> "The world in which many children now grow up is crowded, not necessarily with occupants and not at all with memorable experiences, but with happenings; it is a ceaseless flow of seductive trivialities which invoke neither reflection nor choice but instant participation."[17]

This was written in 1975, the year I graduated from high school, before personal computers, laptops, cell phones, i-anythings, bluetooth, blueray or blue states, before much more than three or four TV stations were available in most places.

---

[17] Michael Oakeshott, *The Voice of Liberal Learning*, page 41, Yale (1989)

One of the common themes in many of these short writings is the importance of meaning conveyed by words alone, in this age of visual images. Words can be used to clarify or to hide meaning, to promote or discourage a thought or idea, to advance or suppress knowledge. Reginald cared passionately about the proper use of words.

Sometimes the power of words is conveyed through other images. I read Antonio Skarmeta's play "Burning Patience" some years before it was used as the basis for the movie "Il Postino." The story is about how Pablo Neruda's Italian mailman became a poet and, ultimately, was killed for being one.

Words have consequences.

Alan Contreras
Eugene, Oregon
June, 2013

The Correspondence

April 22, 2007
Alan to Reginald

Just a note to say that I enjoyed *Fata Morgana*.[18] I particularly like Narcissus to Echo, Turandot, Eve's Awakening and While the Temptations... I have all of your books and very much appreciate your work. I'm a birder and have written some bird books among other things; it is nice to find actual birds instead of generic "seagulls" in your poems (they seem a recent arrival - your partner's influence?) but surely an immature ring-billed gull sets a new standard ! Some years ago there was an uproar in the birding community because in the movie "Jonathan Livingston Seagull," in which a particular gull was supposedly being followed, it not only changed age in the wrong direction but changed species.

I look forward to reading Robert Philen's pieces, which I notice you have linked to on your web site. I am particularly interested in the music one because I recently commented to a friend that I had always disliked Gershwin until I heard a live performance of "American in Paris" several years ago. It seemed astonishingly different from every (disliked) recording I had ever heard, and far, far better. I can't say I have become a Gershwin fan, but now I feel like I understand what Gershwin is supposed to be, and appreciate the music for what it is.

By the way, I mentioned your gloriousness in one of my commentaries in *Inside Higher Education*[19] last summer:

[appropriate segment of that essay inserted below]

"Faculty at the great majority of schools are not really interested in color-coding their potential co-workers on a sepia-index wall chart anyway; they are interested in whether those co-workers are any good. Their departments don't care that Carl Phillips, Yusef Komunyakaa or Reginald Shepherd are black; their co-workers care that they are three

---

[18] Reginald Shepherd, *Fata Morgana (Poems)*, 2007, Pittsburgh.
[19] *Inside Higher Education* - http://www.insidehighered.com/

of the best poets writing in the U.S. today. I hope that nobody at Old Dominion thinks of Adolphus Hailstork as "the black composer in our music department;" they undoubtedly think of him as the composer who wrote "Sonata da Chiesa," one of the best pieces by any composer in a hundred years.

Anyone who tried to recruit these people away on behalf of another school would, I trust, be discreetly shunted off in another direction and told to stop poaching. This is not because they are of color, it is because they are of quality. It is not faculty of color that are such an important example to students of all shades, it is good faculty of color. And there are not enough of them being made."

Best wishes for your continued success.

Alan

April 23, 2007
Reginald to Alan

Dear Alan,

Thank you so much for your note and for your kind words about *Fata Morgana* and my other books. I've realized in the past several years that I'm rather of a landscape poet, and Robert, my partner, is an avid birder and amateur naturalist. He has taught me a lot about the particulars of the landscape and its inhabitants, avian and piscine, both in upstate New York and down here in Pensacola, including the birds at the feeders we used to have. It's been a fascinating new realm for me. I've always been interested in accuracy and in the ballast of fact, and I've always loved the names of things. Learning about these things first hand is only of the many benefits of our relationship.

I read Jonathan Livingston Seagull in the third or fourth grade, I believe. I knew nothing about seagulls, but I was very disappointed that I couldn't meditate or concentrate hard enough to teleport, or whatever it was that he did in the book. I'm sure that if I had known anything about seagulls, I would have [been] irritated by the errors you mention--I was a very pedantic child, and am still a stickler for accuracy.

Robert and I recently saw the Atlanta Symphony Orchestra perform The Rite of Spring, a truly overwhelming piece when heard live (you feel it in your body), and a totally different experience than listening to a recording. We saw the Pensacola Opera do Turandot a few years ago (the inspiration for my poem), a surprisingly good performance for a very small local company, and had the same experience: when Turandot sang "In Questa Reggia" (she was a very powerful singer), my whole body vibrated.

I read your piece in *Inside Higher Education*, and was quite flattered and honored to be listed with Yusef Komunyakaa and Carl Phillips as among the best poets in America today. Unfortunately, though, when I read the piece I was locked in a discrimination battle with the school at which I'd taught here in Pensacola for many years, first as an adjunct and then as a one-year visiting professor. (I got a settlement, enough to sustain myself for a while but insufficient to compensate for what was done to me.) So I felt a strong sense of irony as I read the piece, which obviously had nothing to do with the wonderful things you said, but with the contrast between those much-appreciated comments and the situation I found myself in. I am unfortunately unable to feel very sanguine about the position of black faculty in academia.

Thanks very much for writing and, again, for your very generous words about my work. It's nice to know that when one throws one's rose petal into the Grand Canyon (in David Wojahn's image of publishing a book of poems), someone actually notices.

all best, Reginald

13

Stravinsky's Rite of Spring and the Experience of Art (Musical and Visual)

Robert Philen, posted April 16, 2007.

I had the wonderful experience this past weekend of watching and hearing Robert Spano and the Atlanta Symphony perform Igor Stravinsky's *The Rite of Spring*. I have listened to recordings of this piece many, many times, but hearing and seeing it performed live for the first time, I began to understand some of the extreme reactions (including negative reactions) some have to the work, both at its premier in 1913 and subsequently. (I'm also aware that part of the initial reaction at the premier in 1913 was to the "scandalous" visual aspects of the ballet which the music accompanied – but I also suspect then and later, that the seemingly unusual qualities of the music had a lot to do with the violently negative reaction.)

I'd like here to address two topics having to do with the experience of art musical and visual: (1) the differences in experience of live musical performance or original works of art versus the experience of reproductions (whether recordings of music or prints or photographs of visual art); and (2) a greater conservatism apparent with regard to audiences for music compared to audiences for visual art. *"Live" vs. Facsimile* There is a difference between the experience of music performed live and the experience of recorded music. (There is also music that blurs the difference, such as live performance which incorporates taped material – and there are both "high" and "low" art versions of this.)

While it doesn't seem quite right to refer to the experience of an original painting or sculpture as a "live" experience (though that description would certainly apply to visual performance art), there is a difference between seeing an original work and a reproduction (though here too, there is art that blurs the distinction, e.g. Warhol's camouflage screen prints, or mass produced casts of Rodin's sculptures).

In the case of both music and visual art, there are differences between individual pieces in the degree to which the experience of the live performance or original work is different from the experience of a facsimile. Large scale paintings or sculpture feel far different in person than in photographic

14

reproduction in even the best art books, as do highly textured paintings, where the texture is not reproducible in the flat two dimensional page.

On the program with The Rite of Spring were also Stravinsky's "Dumbarton Oaks" concerto for chamber orchestra and Mozart's piano concerto no. 17, with piano soloist Garrick Ohlsson. While I enjoyed the performance of these two pieces, the main difference in experiencing them live was in seeing what the musicians were physically doing at any moment, while my physical experience of *The Rite of Spring* was completely different from that I have ever experienced while listening to it on CD.

This brings me to a major difference in the experience of visual art and music. The difference between seeing an original painting and a reproduction is not the same as the difference between a live performance of music and a recording. The difference between the visual experience of an original visual work and a facsimile is primarily a quantitative one. One sees more of the texture, the size, the other details indicating the skill of a painter or sculptor. The experience of live music also involves such quantitative differences, but a qualitative difference in experience as well. Looking at a painting and looking at a reproduction of it, while producing different specific sensations, are the same sorts of experiences. Listening to live and recorded music provide similar sorts of auditory experiences, but live music can also provide a distinct bodily experience rarely provided by recorded music played over speakers. This is especially so with high volume live music, or live performance involving especially deep, resonant pitches that are experienced in a literally visceral way, experienced bodily in the gut as much as in the ear.

Conservatism in Musical Experience

A few years ago, my local symphony orchestra, the Pensacola Symphony Orchestra, also performed *The Rite of Spring*. I'm ashamed to admit I missed the performance – I don't even remember why any longer, but afterwards, according to one member of the orchestra I spoke with, the Pensacola symphony received several letters of complaint about the choice to program this piece of "cacophonous non-music." I was aghast at the time that anyone would have reacted this way – *The Rite of Spring* has been standard repertory for almost a century now. While tempting to pass this off as the backward taste of provincial rubes, I've also encountered similar musical conservatism in other places (for example, I've encountered numerous writings attempting to dismiss Schoenberg or Berg as "cacophonous" or "snarling dissonance" – a reaction I find both wrongheaded and simply inaccurate [dissonance sure, as in any interesting music, but no snarling or cacophony]), and as I said above, after hearing the piece live, while I find it even more than before one of the most profound pieces of 20th century music, I can begin to understand others' visceral reactions against the piece (in part because it is a literally visceral reaction).

The experience of visual art or of music is different from the experience of literature. Literature also presents a unique object to be experienced (with this being especially a goal of poetry). But the experience of literature requires active participation of the reader in a way that visual art and music do not. One cannot simply pass by a book and experience anything of it the way one could with a painting or a musical performance. Instead it has to be intentionally picked up and read, and the experience of it is a distinctly interior one.

Paintings, sculpture, and music are experienced as things more clearly exterior than literature, with the experience occurring somewhat more passively (one can actively look or listen, but one can't easily not see something that passes through one's field of vision and one can't easily not hear something within auditory range), with the object impinging upon one's senses from outside. At the same time, there is a difference in this exterior, passive experience of visual art and music. Visual art is more exterior, and not at all visceral in any literal way. It is only seen, where live music is heard *and* felt, experienced as something distinctly exterior while also something distinctly resonating in one's physical being.

One can also more easily stop experiencing painting or sculpture – by closing one's eyes or looking in another direction, while music cannot be tuned out so simply. It impinges on one's ears and body, and it cannot be ignored. It can force itself upon a person in a way that visual art (much less literature) cannot. As a result, music can be physically delightful – or a physical shock and violation if the music is not to one's liking.

Many were once shocked by modernist experiments in sculpture and painting. Some perhaps still are, but really only very few can still honestly profess to be shocked or disturbed by Duchamp, or Picasso, or Pollock (much less the impressionists). But *The Rite of Spring* remains physically exhilarating or frightening or both at once.

Reading, Looking, Listening

Robert Philen, posted April 25, 2007 .

In a recent post, "Stravinsky's Rite of Spring and the Experience of Art (Musical and Visual)," and in the comments section attached to that post, I argued that the experience of literature is different in some ways from that of visual art or music. I'd like here to explore and clarify this distinction a bit further. The experience of visual art or music involves looking or listening, each of which entails direct sensory perception of external phenomena that can impinge themselves upon us without our choosing – we experience *something* simply by being in the presence of the visual or auditory object. To experience something that is not superficial of a sculpture, painting, photograph or piece of music, of course requires more than this – *active* looking or listening involving concentration, contemplation, and conceptualization.

Reading literature (or anything else) is always operating already at the sort of second order level we see with active looking and listening. Reading involves and is built upon looking, but looking alone isn't reading. The sensory experience of a book or computer screen and the visual qualities of letters and words aren't text (i.e. the page isn't the text).

Text is always something created internally by contemplation and conception (e.g. seeing that "A," "a," "*a*," or "**A**," look different is direct sensory experience of visual phenomena – recognizing any or all of them as "the letter A" involves internal conception and interpretation), albeit prompted by and in relation to the *concrete* visual qualities of the page ("the letter A" can only be recognized in relation to a limited range of visual phenomena) much in the same way that active listening or looking involve inner contemplation in relation to distinctly external phenomena.

April 23, 2007
Alan to Reginald

Great to hear from you, and thanks for writing. I'm sorry that you had to read my *Inside Higher Ed* piece under such unpleasant conditions. I read both of Robert's pieces, very good. I think one of the things that made the live Gershwin so much better than the recordings was that I could almost feel the air rushing out of the instruments past me, it was indeed a much more physical experience.

Before I forget, the University of Oregon has a temporary appointment in poetry coming up in the creative writing program. Not sure how temporary or whether it could morph into permanent; I asked my spies today and that is all I have back so far. I hope UO was not the northwest school where you had a previous unpleasant experience. I'm afraid the UO is sometimes rather clumsy in how it deals with "minorities." They are absolutely sloshing with Good Intentions. However, I have very good contacts there from my previous job and would be glad to fish for information if you have any interest. Not sure what Robert's professional situation is.

As for your work, my local bookstore has a standing order for new works by only three poets: you, Carl Phillips and J.D. McClatchy - who have little in common but speak to different parts of me. I buy Komunyakaa from time to time, and lots of others. Among the dead, I return most often to Auden and James Merrill. Among translations, Pessoa, sometimes Gabriela Mistral and, when I was younger, Neruda. I need to get back to Neruda sometime.

I also support poetry when I can. Last year I underwrote a friend of mine's first collection in a very nice small run. It seems to me that those of us who believe in the value of the fine arts need to take personal action to support them, not wait for somebody else to do it.

Have you ever read a poem - really a series - called David and Jonathan, by Byron Herbert Reece? From a book called *Bow Down in Jericho*.[20] Came out in 1950. Extraordinary. I am talking

---

[20] Byron Herbert Reece, *Bow Down in Jericho*, 1950. 1985 printing, Cherokee, Atlanta (Marietta).

with a local artist and publisher about bringing it out in a joint illustrated edition with Pessoa's "Antinous," which as far as I know has never been issued in the U.S.[21]

I appreciate your comment about facts as ballast. I think that's exactly the right place for them. I enjoy the poetry of Pattiann Rogers, but sometimes I feel as though I am drowning in terminology and I lose the poem. I have an acquaintance whose poetry is often quite good, but in one poem he included the words "ootheca" and "blattarian," perfectly real words related to insects, but I prodded him for it in a review I did for one of our local mini-mags. What does one do with that kind of language, anyway? I got this little ditty in my head, after which the poem was hopeless:

I wanta put my pecka
Inside of yo' ootheca

I am a poet of quite modest gifts (see above), but I enjoy writing poetry. Doing it well takes considerable focus and concentration. I think I do better in essays. That may be partly a matter of habit and practice, as I have been writing a lot of essays in recent years because they pay, which poetry usually doesn't. Here's to filthy lucre !

Are you and Robert aware that there is a gay birders national e-mail chatlist? We host each other and organize trips, etc. My friends Michael Retter and Rich Hoyer are among those who operate it. There is a large clutch of members in Atlanta called The Gaggle.

My yard is very shrubby and right now I have migrant Golden-crowned and White-crowned Sparrows (we get only a few White-throated here), plus a pair of Bushtits creeping around looking for a nest site. We're just getting the front edge of orioles, flycatchers and tanagers this week.

I seem to have written a whole story here, so I'll stop.

Alan

---

[21] *Antinous* was written originally in English, is in the public domain and is published as an appendix herein.

Alan Contreras
Three short reviews

David Laing, Passage (Traprock, Eugene, 2002)
Michael Spring, Edge of Blue (Siski, Corvallis, 2002)
Hannah Wilson, The Habit of Digging (Bella, Eugene, 2002)

These reviews focus on three recent chapbooks by Willamette Valley poets. That such unassuming microfibers in the great tapestry of poetry can sometimes prove the most lasting strands of all is perhaps obvious: I will mention only Dickinson and Cavafy. All three of these Oregon poets have been a presence in northwest writing for many years, and all three booklets show that experience. Otherwise they represent three very different styles, both of presentation and of content.

It is easy to refer to David Laing's "Passage" as nature poetry, but even in recent decades the arms of that goddess have encompassed a vast flock of naturophiles from the brooding bone-tapper Loren Eiseley to the celebratory Linnaean Pattiann Rogers. Laing's approach is delicate without losing strength, not the easiest task, and his themes are familiar without being tedious: the movements of geese, the rise and fall of waters, hawks on the hunt and herons on the watch.

These poems and their subjects are clearly inhabitants of western Oregon; Laing's are poems of place, not just symbols bolted onto a natural frame. Wendell Berry writes of the mind being "at home on its native ground," and that calm sense of belonging, an unfeigned connection with the nearby natural world, is the great strength of "Passage."

The writing is measured and spare, the presentation more akin to Basho than to any modern American who leaps to mind, Merwin at his least mystic and some of Gary Snyder perhaps excepted. These words flow so well that there seem to be more than are actually present, witness the concluding section from "Prey," in which a familiar hawk greets the poet:

I am not prepared
  when she decides
    drops from the sky

swoops

comes closer each time
  aiming I realize

for the heart

A poet appreciative of the beauty of our surroundings can sometimes allow the flow of descriptive language to uproot lighter facts and carry them out of sight. The reference to "rosy finches" resting in a madrone in "Farmer Creek/Meditation" is an example. Rosy finches are birds of subalpine rocks such as Steens Mountain and the Three Sisters, wintering in open spaces, thus they will rarely see a madrone tree, an ornithological quibble which detracts little from the overall enjoyment of this volume.

Michael Spring's "Edge of Blue" is a more varied collection and contains more people than finches. This is not a visit to a familiar place, rather a view of things familiar and unfamiliar from unusual angles. There is a lot that snaps and crackles in this collection, the work of a poet who has not only an exceptional command of language but the ability to see ordinary events from points no one else would think of.

The extraordinary variance in viewpoint and tone in this collection makes for a swooping ride from the dark challenge of boxing gloves prepared (to settle a father-son argument?) but never used:

...
when he visits
his father never talks about them
but they are always in the room
...

to the startling "licking the corn field," which begins:

I know I shouldn't have
done that — now I'm stuck
pulling crows from my tongue
like burrs from socks

This is a truly original voice generating a full spectrum of visions from an astonishing variety of viewpoints. Many modern poets—even many good ones—work mainly within a certain unstated framework of experience, topics and issues. Few are able to see so much of what the world really contains (or might contain) as Michael Spring.

Sometimes his desire to work with a specific reality sails into shoal water: one poem contains the words "ootheca" and "blattarian" in less than three lines. I was not sure whether to reach for the dictionary or the eyedrops. Such pulsing objects dredged from the scientific abyss argue for a poetic catch-and-release program: they add veracity and color but at too great a cost to readability. It is a tribute to Spring's ability that even this poem fought free of its lexical quicksand and became an unusual view of, yes, cockroaches, which emerge

like a gang of young teens
having crawled out of their bedroom
windows to meet in the park

an embryotic molt
...

This collection contains such an exceptional variety of interesting, well-written poems that anyone who wants to read the best of Oregon poetry should get a copy before they disappear.

The preceding two collections are written by observers looking, for the most part, at others or at the natural world. The late Hannah Wilson's "The Habit of Digging" is more introspective, visiting pockets of personal and family history with a clear eye and the advantages that come from a lifetime of careful observation, self-awareness and attention to language.

Two of the best poems in this collection link a past and present event, e.g. remembrance of a girlhood riding her bicycle away from New York City is brought back by the sight of a more modern yet corroded bike on the beach, insufficient to carry the weight of time:

I want to ride this uncomplicated,
back-road vehicle back
into those still-lifes. But the bike is rusted,

the tires flat, and the sand softens,
the later it gets.

Likewise, "The White Sweater" links the touch of a sweater found at a modern store to one she wore fifty years ago when her body was suddenly becoming that of a woman—a body that has changed once again:

I don't have room for this sweater I want
to wear away the imposed shame,
to atone to my severed breasts for my betrayal.

Knowing the poet as one of my English teachers from many years ago, I find most stirring "The Teacher," which begins with her comment on an ill-chosen obituary, presumably for a friend, and concludes with these words about a teacher known to be difficult:

But through every cold season, a few,
boys and girls, hung upon her arms unshaken.
They followed her home for seminars in Milton,
and when she'd made the darkness visible,
they carried in her firewood.

What more moving poem has ever been written of a teacher? This poem has a old-school silverprint quality, an image clear and yet possessed of gradations that take additional looks before they can be seen. Such are many of the poems in this collection, the shortest of the three but the richest in human experience and perhaps in wisdom.

Fireweed 13(1), 2002

May 1, 2007
Reginald to Alan

Dear Alan,

Thanks for your note, and sorry I've taken a bit to get back to you. I went to the emergency room with excruciating abdominal pains the day before you wrote, spent most of the next day sleeping, and have been feeling sick on and off (mostly on) ever since. I'm supposed to see a specialist tomorrow who will hopefully be able to find out what's going on and (more importantly) how to make it stop.

I'm glad that you liked Robert's pieces. I think that he's quite brilliant, but there's a slight possibility that I'm biased. :-) I don't see live music much, but especially for classical music, the physical presence of the music and the music-making is utterly incomparable with the experience of listening to a recording.

UO was definitely not the Northwestern school I was referring to in my race and academia post; that was Evergreen State College. UO certainly seems like a good school, but Robert has a tenure-track job teaching anthropology here that he likes and I couldn't ask him to give it up for a temporary position. Nor would we be willing to live apart even for a semester. I know that's not typical of academics, but I put my life first, and however I make a living (very badly, at the moment), my career is my writing as a poet and critic, not as an academic, though I would definitely like to have a permanent academic position, for the health benefits even more than for the salary (as an HIV positive person, access to health care is crucial for me). But I do greatly appreciate your thinking of me and mentioning the possibility to me.

I'm flattered to be one of three poets for whose work you have a standing order. I read with Yusef Komunyakaa about ten years ago, when I lived in Chicago, but when I saw him at AWP he didn't seem to remember me. Oh well. Actually, I read with Carl too then, and Kevin Young. I've not read much Neruda in a while, but I was recently listening to Samuel Barber's *The Lovers*, which sets several pieces from Neruda's *Twenty Love Poems and a Song of Despair*; it's a beautiful piece of music.

I have never heard of Byron Herbert Reece. Perhaps, with the aid of the Internet (good sometimes for other things besides buying stuff), I will try to look him up.

24

I love facts and things and lists of things, and sometimes I have to remind myself to maintain a balance between loading every rift with ore, as Keats put it, though I'm using the phrase a bit more literally, and overloading the ship to the point at which it just won't float (pardon my mixed metaphors).

We don't have many birds in the yards of our new house (we've been in this house for almost two years, after renting a house for four years), mostly mockingbirds and brown thrashers, occasional cardinals and mourning doves, and once or twice a bluejay. There were some robins passing through a while ago. At the old house we had lots of bird feeders, but the squirrels were always getting at them and it drove me insane. I kept buying different kinds of feeders hoping to keep them away, putting out traps which just killed the slower, stupider squirrels (I realized that I was selecting for the smarter, stronger ones, and stopped), and mixing the seeds with squirrel repellent (cayenne pepper), which some of them decided they liked. There aren't as many suitable places to hang the feeders around this new house, and we decided it was probably best if I didn't have a fit every five minutes (I used to run out into the yard chasing the squirrels with sticks). But we do have blackberries all over the yards, front, back, and side. Robert picks them every day and there are still more.

I am getting a bit tired and so will sign off for now. Take good care.

peace and poetry, Reginald

May 01, 2007
Alan to Reginald

Yow, that ailment doesn't sound like much fun. Granted, we do leave our bodies behind eventually (as a nonbeliever I find this quite unreasonable and distressing), but to live in a body that is biting back really seems unfair. Let me know when you are about to turn 50 (I'm 51) and I'll tell you The Truth About Your Upcoming Colonoscopy. You are what, 40ish?

Robert is a good writer, clear and understandable, which is appallingly rare among professors. I've added his blog to the very short list that I look at now and then.

25

Evergreen, oy. Quite a decent place, really, but so detached from norms that they sometimes think they operate in their own universe. If I may be permitted an improper joke (impropriety being one of my strengths), they're so Green they can't figure out what to do with any other color. UO is not as much that way, though there is a pulsing core of people in and around the university who go through life looking for opportunities to be offended, and who of course profess their tolerance for all. Sometimes they remind me of that old Phil Ochs song "Love me, I'm a Liberal." It's a scream if you've never heard it.

I'm going to attach my working copy of the hypothetical "special edition" of Pessoa's "Antinous" and Reece's "David and Jonathan." It includes my own intro, which can be ignored as the idle vaporings of the uninformed, and the text of both. I find both of these extraordinary, in different ways. Reece has a peculiar old world village-prophet feel to him—I can almost smell oil lamps and a goat—which in clumsy hands would fall somewhere between humorous and unfortunate. I find his hands remarkably deft. Jonathan starts out plain, almost flat, and suddenly turns to pure fire on the page—I can't think of another poem that, to my ear, has such a huge transition in tone. Made me sit straight up in the chair and think "holy shit!" I would be very interested in what you think of his work.

I'm reading Edward Hirsch's *The demon and the angel*[22] now. So far very good. After that the biography of Neruda, which will take a while. Would you like to do a reading here maybe a year from now? I can probably arrange the swag to cover it.

And in matters truly important, I can recommend, after years of searching, an effective anti-squirrel feeder ! I'll get you the name of it when it isn't pouring rain (hey, it's Oregon).

Take care of yourself. We need more work from you !

Alan

---

[22] Edward Hirsch, *The demon and the angel*, 2002. Harcourt.

May 5, 2007
Reginald to Alan

Dear Alan,

I am forty-four this April and have already experienced all too much of my body's betrayal. I try to treat my body right (I feed it good food, I exercise it, I try to give it enough sleep and rest, I avoid stress as much as I can) and it repays me with pain. I saw a urologist on Wednesday and he explained that I have uric acid kidney stones which, unlike calcified stones, can be treated medically, with potassium supplements to make my urine less acid and more alkaline. I've just started them today. I try to hydrate myself, but I am also embarking upon a project of constant hydration. I hope that these two things will take care of that problem. As for my constant fatigue, that still requires investigation.

One of Robert's parents has had a colonoscopy, and what they say at least they put you under for it. If I were ever to undergo such a procedure, I would insist on being knocked out for it.

Robert does indeed stand out from the pack, in just about every way. I'm glad that you're enjoying his blog.

I would quite love to do a reading at U of Oregon if you could swing the swag. I do quite like that word, "swag." It makes me think of money swaggering, which in our profit-driven world I suppose it does.

Do let me know the name of your effective anti-squirrel feeder when you get a chance. Right now, though, I'm concerned about a much more serious rodent problem. Last night I saw a rat (a large rat) crawling across a pipe of some kind above the garage door and into a hole in the ceiling leading to the attic. Robert assures me that a) that part of the attic contains only insulation and is completely sealed off from the finished attic that we actually use and from the rest of the house and b) that country rats are not aggressive like city rats, and are in general outdoor creatures. Why then is [it] in the attic of our garage? And rats can chew, through walls even. I am quite thoroughly freaked out. I grew up with rats and I have a pretty comprehensive phobia. Robert bought a rat trap (Wal-Mart had only one) and put out poison in the garage, but we need to call an exterminator. We need to have them completely gone or I will never be able to rest easy in this house again.

On that cheerful note, I will sign off. I am feeling much better, but in part because I've been so sick and lethargic, have fallen behind on a ton of things I need to be doing and have no desire to do. Speaking of things I do want to do, I'm looking forward to reading the poems you sent me.

Take good care.

all best, Reginald

The Experience of Live Music

Robert Philen, posted June 19, 2007.

I've written in two previous posts about the experience of music, especially live performance and including how the experience of music or listening compares with other art forms, e.g. the experiences of visual art through looking or of literature through reading (see "Stravinsky's Rite of Spring and the Experience of Art [Musical and Visual]" and "Reading, Looking, Listening"). About a week ago I had the pleasure of witnessing a phenomenal performance of Carl Orff's *Carmina Burana* by the Atlanta Symphony Orchestra. In light of that experience, I'd like to raise two points for discussion as an addendum to those earlier posts.

Watching Music

Obviously music per se can't be watched – it's comprised of sound. But the physical performance of the music by live musicians can be. The theatricality of a rock show is as much about the visual performance of the band, a light show, etc. While not typically involving things like laser light shows, watching the musicians play is an important component of experiencing live jazz or classical music or any other music. One of the most engaging aspects of watching live music is the way that visual clues can cue you in to subtle aspects of the music otherwise not noticed.

In *Carmina Burana*, in addition to the full orchestra and chorus, there are three vocal soloists: a soprano, tenor, and baritone. The tenor only sings one song (a lament for a cooked swan), and in the case of this song, the singer is accompanied primarily by the viola section. Before seeing the piece live, I had actually not particularly noticed the violas nor the subtle beauty of the music being played in that section of the music. I'm not sure why I had never noticed before – maybe I've always just focused in on the tenor's voice in that song, but it was initially seeing the physical actions of the violists' bowing (while most of the rest of the orchestra sat still) that made me focus my attention on that component of the music.

For me, and I think for most music lovers, this aspect of musical experience is one of the main reasons and joys to experiencing music live. Hearing Live Music in Relation to Recorded Music As Claude Lévi-Strauss discussed in the "Overture" section of *The Raw and the Cooked* (and as I discussed in my essay "Reflections on Meaning and Myth: Claude Lévi-Strauss Revisited," *Anthropos*, 2005, V. 100: 221 – 228), music offers an experience that is simultaneously diachronic and synchronic. It unfolds through time (hence the diachronic) – music is largely about our experience of time – but it is simultaneously experienced as if all at once (hence the synchronic) in the sense that what is experienced at any moment is experienced in relation to the memory of what has gone before and the anticipation that sets up about the still unfolding music – with much of the joy of the experience of music coming from the way in which the music meets our expectation or does not and surprises us. It is through this combination of diachronic and synchronic experience that music actively engages the mind.

Over the past century of so, recordings have upped the ante. Before the prevalence of recorded music, the only way to experience music was via live performance. This limited (though it did not eliminate – especially in the case of "folk" genres that would have been more familiar to most people) the ability of people to "know" the piece of music being played before its performance. It's now possible to enter into a live performance of most music of any genre with a thorough knowledge of what that music usually sounds like. This has had multiple effects. Many histories of classical music that I have read indicate that one effect of this has been to raise the expectations of audiences and to raise performance standards for musicians and orchestras. When avid (and even not so avid in the case of particularly famous pieces of music) fans enter the performance with a thorough sense of how the music is "supposed to" sound, the bar is raised. In general, this is a good thing, though it might also increase the chances of disappointment from perfectly adequate performances that might simply not reach the highest pinnacles of performance of the last century.

Some worry that the prevalence of recording has homogenized performance. This is to some extent true, e.g. distinct national styles of instrumental or vocal performance are much less in evidence in classical music than was true several decades ago. At the same time, to some extent the presence of so many recordings of repertoire pieces encourages diversity of interpretation.

If you're going to record *yet another* interpretation of *Carmina Burana* at this point, you ought to present something new in the piece. An example of this is Simon Rattle's recent recording of the piece – his pacing to me seems a bit too fast for the work to enjoy listening to too often, but he definitely presents a distinct interpretation the distinctiveness of which would be apparent to most people even casually familiar with the work.

Entering the experience already familiar with multiple recordings of *Carmina Burana*, I had high standards for the piece (which were abundantly met). Further, though, having the memory of pre-existing experiences with the piece (and with the Atlanta Symphony under Robert Spano and with other performances of other pieces I've experienced by this symphony), my experience and pleasure was heightened by the recognition of particular aspects of interpretation that made this particular performance distinct.

In this case (as with the performance of Stravinsky's *Rite of Spring* I enjoyed earlier this spring), in certain movements the percussion was prominently emphasized. (Both *Carmina Burana* and *The Rite of Spring* are highly percussive in places in any interpretation, but this was more prominent than in most.) As a result, I noticed certain percussive elements, e.g. the almost machine-gun-like snare drum in the early moments of the piece, that I'd never particularly noticed before – and that experience now informs each further experience of the piece, whether live or recorded.

May 8, 2007
Alan to Reginald

I was fishing around in Robert's blog and found several pieces on music in addition to the one on live vs unlive performances. I don't have his e-mail so am sending you a little piece that I did recently. It is nothing special but he might enjoy it.

I think the transition from family musical lives lived jointly (generally true until the early 20th Century) and today's utterly splintered musical lives in which parents haven't the slightest idea what their children listen to or why, is an underappreciated cultural change in American life.

Alan

Alan Contreras
Ned Rorem and the future of American song

I am not sure why I did not come across the writing and music of Ned Rorem until I was 47. I had seen his name occasionally over the years with no particular spark. A couple of years ago a reference to one of his diaries—I can't even remember where I saw it—finally registered with enough effect and I dug up a used copy of the *New York Diary* at a local bookstore. By the time I was 30 pages into it I knew that I would have to read all of them, and listen to his music. I have now read many of his books and own several of his music CDs.

The recent release of both his latest set of essays (*Facing the Night*, Shoemaker & Hoard 2006), a collection of his letters to various famous and less famous people (*Wings of Friendship*, Shoemaker & Hoard 2005) and not long ago a collection of his earlier works (*A Ned Rorem Reader*, Yale 2001) provides an opportunity to look at his life works as a whole. I have to say "works" rather than "work" because Rorem, in his own words, is a generalist in the European mode, not an American-style narrow specialist. He does more than one thing well.

Rorem is frustrated at the prospect of being remembered more as a writer than as a composer. I lost track of the number of times in his writing that he declaims "I am a composer who also writes, not a writer who also composes." But that is not how history works, and history won't weigh in with any definitive trends for another twenty years or so.

It might be more accurate to say that his writing is likely to survive *in toto* as a body of literature read and discussed for decades to come, while his music is likely to be remembered in bits and pieces, with much of it fading out over time. Yet that is what happens to most composers and to most music. If it does not happen to all of his music and all of his written work, he will be among the rare few.

For example, who outside Australia knows well the gorgeous work of Colin Brumby, whose Symphony No. 1, flute and clarinet works and Piano Concerto ought to be played by all of the world's major orchestras? Is Shaun Davey, whose Relief of Derry Symphony and Granuaile song cycle deserve great acclaim, a household word in the musical community outside the Celtic world? How many American concertgoers have heard the splendid Sonata da Chiesa of Adolphus Hailstork, from our own country? Who now hears performances of the Swedish master Ture Rangstrom?

Music is a world in which "modern" has become synonymous with "unpleasant," which leads orchestras wanting an audience into the closed loop of miscellaneous dead Germanic tunemongers, with an admixture of other dead Europeans (what to call them – a froth of French, a roulade of Russians, a briskness of Brits?) and only the occasional living composer, generally the unpleasant ones. There are exceptions to the rule of modern unpleasantness: in addition to Brumby, Davey and Hailstork, John Tavener, Arvo Part, the late Lee Hoiby and William Hawley come quickly to mind.

Rorem is fortunate in that during his lifetime his music has been played fairly often, and some of his work that capsized instantly upon completion (e.g. his First and Second symphonies) has been refloated with considerable approbation. The Bournemouth Symphony recently released the first commercial recording of those two symphonies (as well as the Third, which had a brief life thirty years ago) directed by Jose Serebrier, and these works are astonishingly fresh and full of zing, a perfect blend of identifiable melody and modern intonation. This recording was nominated for three Grammys.

Rorem asks that he be first judged as a composer and I can say that I am very glad he is one, because his best works, e.g. some of those for flute, are likely to last for a while and have certainly brought me a lot of pleasure. That is all most composers can expect. Nonetheless, I think the diaries will, over time, be viewed as a unique literary masterpiece, burning in the dim corridors of historic time with a brighter flame than the music.

What is it about these diaries that makes them so appealing? There is a certain flavor of celebrity, of course, since Rorem (still composing and reasonably spry at 88 as I write this) fell in with a lot of well-known people in Paris, New York and elsewhere in the 1950s. Hearing of his interactions with people such as Jean Cocteau, Edward Albee and Leonard Bernstein, often when the Famous Person was not yet famous or was just getting to be known, has a certain sparkle. Rorem's willingness to state the, how can I put it, bare facts as he saw them, even when those facts are a bit more colorful or just more visible than what we usually see, adds spice to the overall tone.

Most of all, there is a sense of seeing sixty years of history open leaf by leaf, progress season by season. It is simultaneously a personal history, a history of 20th Century music and a broader history of changes in American society, all at once, like the twining of cultural DNA from one horizon to the other, with some recognizable patterns but a lot of change and unique perceptions.

In its personal aspect, the diaries are also a history of gay culture. Rorem grew up in an unusual environment for the mid-century in that his Quaker parents were apparently not too troubled by the fact that he was gay, or at least accepted it with grace. It is interesting to compare his relatively open experiences to the more constricted social beginnings of contemporaries Gore Vidal and James Merrill. Vidal grew up inside the American political establishment, choosing to write for a living (a living that was a little sparse from time to time) rather than accept the horror of teaching. Merrill did not really have to work for a living (Merrill as in Merrill Lynch) but became a respected and prolific poet. Both became open about their sexuality in a rather careful, restrained manner, though Vidal wrote about homosexual attractions early in his career.

Rorem, on the other hand, wrote matter-of-factly about the joys and disappointments of his own activity chasing men decades before such revelations were common. He did not belabor the issue, it was just part of his life so it came up naturally in his writings without taking over the story. It is that matter-of-factness that makes these works stand out in the period in which they were written.

What I find most resonant about Rorem's diaries is his frequent descriptions of how the creative process works (or doesn't work). He does not discuss the process of writing music in much detail, but the various issues that any creative person faces, and the peculiar misconceptions of friends and family about that process, make for a table-pounding "right on!" sort of reading experience. The fact that I am also a gay person raised in Quaker meeting, as he was, makes this sense of having found a philosophical uncle all the more rewarding.

A good example of his perfect evocation of the necessities of the creative process can be found where he refers to a friend

35

who thought that the sights and sounds of Morocco must have been a great inspiration to his work, since he did so much early work there while vacationing, in a manner of speaking, from his nominal residence in southern France.

In fact, the great advantage of working in Morocco, in addition to a Gide-like exploration of the joys of young male Moroccans, was that no one could find him or distract him there, so he could pull the shades against the glories of Morocco and actually get some composing done. This is precisely the experience and reaction that I have had and that many of my friends who write and paint have had, to which I can only say "preach it, brother Ned."

For anyone who wants to experience the extraordinary breadth of human experience, including the greatest joys and the most horrifying losses, through the eyes and ears of a great writer and great composer, read the saga of Ned Rorem in his own words, and listen to the generations of songs, symphonies and other music that this unique American voice has brought us.

Returning to the world of American song in which Rorem was the leading composer for many years, I listen and I hear a universe utterly changed, and yet there are niches in which song, in a form that Rorem would recognize, though different from his own, is flowering.

A few years ago I heard the University of Oregon's all-male singing group "On the Rocks" while driving home one night. Local station KLCC played their version of Dire Straits' 'Romeo and Juliet' and I had no idea who was singing or where this amazing a cappella version of the song had come from. I called the station and they said that it was a local group called On the Rocks. The station had a CD but seemed to have no idea where it had come from or where to get it.

The next day I went into a music store near the University and mumbled something to the clerk about the song. Before I was finished with my incoherent tale of music found and perhaps lost, he said "On the Rocks" and got a copy of their debut CD off the rack for me. These CDs had been flying out the door all morning, and turned out to be the highest-selling CD for the store all spring. I personally bought a dozen as gifts and an additional fifteen for people at my office who had heard my copy. In an extraordinary violation of professional norms, I even called my staff into my office on some pretense, closed the door and played it for them on my computer's reasonably good speakers.

What is so special about OTR, as they are often called? When I first heard and saw them, the group consisted of nine men ranging in age from 18 to 22, and they sing songs. Well, so do lots of groups. Someone who had not heard them asked me "is that, like, barbershop?" Ah, no. In fact when I invited one of the members whom I knew slightly to the regional barbershop contest—held about five blocks from his house—he answered with great courtesy that he did not think any of the members would be interested.

College musical groups are common. A cappella is much less common, though becoming more so, and least common of all is for a group of young singers to make their own splendid arrangements of very recent popular songs—sometimes songs that had only been on the radio in the original version for a matter of months—retaining the original content of the song but adding their own unique silk and fire to produce something that the university's other singing groups simply describe with the phrase "they're hot."

Today there are other such groups nearby; I recently heard the UO women's group Divisi, Southern Oregon University's Dulcet and Oregon State University's Outspoken. Many other colleges have them: for an astonishing listening experience, buy a copy from iTunes of Leonard Cohen's "Hallelujah" performed by Northwestern University's group 'Freshman Fifteen'. This, their own arrangement, simply assassinates most other performances—and there are dozens. Buy the whole CD. Groups at Yale, Cornell and Michigan have been especially good in recent years.

OTR has made their own arrangements of the song "Hear You Me," originally by Jimmy Eat World, "Demons" by Guster, "Street Spirit" by Radiohead, Cohen's "Hallelujah" and "In the End" by Linkin Park, as well as "Romeo and Juliet" and others. They have also recorded Gounod's "Ave Maria" and Billy Joel's touching "Lullaby." I had never heard many of these songs before I heard the OTR versions; indeed I did not know that many of these musical groups existed. Why not? Because I am, musically, an old person at 55.

Even if I had known of them, I would not have listened to their music, simply because people do not generally listen to popular music except for that of their own generation and, if unavoidable, of their children's generation. Since I have no children and do not own a television, there is no venue in which I would hear this music. So at the very least the transliteration effect of my local singing groups OTR and Divisi has allowed me to experience music that I never would have heard. Barbershop, which my brother sings and I enjoy in moderation, is essentially a fixed style. Its generational crossover is more limited than that of the collegiate acappella groups, which are the true transfer agents of modern American song.

Rorem has commented that it is inappropriate to compare the new music of his generation (generally, the first half of the 20th century, perhaps including the 1950s) to modern popular music because the former is, if you will, classical, while the latter is not. Thus he objects to, for example, comparing Aaron Copland and Bob Dylan because of the nature of their music in a technical sense. I follow this argument and agree with it up to a point, but the question and its answer needs to take into account the changing role of music and songs in society.

My late mother was exactly Ned Rorem's age; she was born one day later. In her youth, adults knew lots of songs from earlier days as well as from their own generation, and in general young people heard the same songs as adults, whether they learned them or not.

My great-grandmother's Liberty Chorus Song Book, issued in 1919 by McKinley Music Co. of Chicago, was used by my grandmother's family and recently came to me. Its editor, Anne Shaw Faulkner, also author of "Music in the Home," closed her introduction to the Liberty Chorus songs with the following declaration about a man returning from World War I: "he will want to sing and to have his loved ones sing at home, at school and in all community gatherings."

These were not only pre-headphone years but almost pre-radio years, with limited offerings available. The first commercial radio station was licensed in 1920, only three years before my mother was born. The phonograph, today almost an artifact, had just switched to "long-play" 33 rpm vinyl from hard 78 rpm "breakables" in my childhood. It was first patented in 1877, so two generations before my mother's had heard music either only as live performances or as families listening to early discs. Listening to music on phonographs required electricity (not uniformly available in rural areas) and quite a bit of effort since the discs were hardly compact: the ones I saw at my grandmother's home were about half an inch thick and contained very little music, requiring multiple discs for even shorter pieces.

Today, members of the same family typically have separate musical lives, and the song, as a "high" art form that Rorem knew and wrote for to great effect, has largely been supplanted by the song designed to appeal either to everyone (often in the form of advertising jingles) or to a specific target audience (country, rock, rap). Loved ones generally don't sing together at home or anywhere else, let alone at community gatherings.

If a single vocal form that meets the esthetic needs of all generations can be found today, it is a cappella singing by truly creative groups like OTR and its collegiate compatriots. Once when I attended an OTR/Divisi show, the age range in my own contingent of about 15 people was nine to 83, and the entire audience reflected this astonishing mix. I do not see that cross-generational appeal (outside music schools) elsewhere in vocal music.

Reginald Shepherd and Robert Philen point out that the pendulum of music may be swinging back somewhat as parents who grew up in the 1960s and 70s are more interested in their children's music of the late 90s and early 2000s than was true for several previous decades. This is a good sign if it proves to be true.

Before OTR became well known at the University of Oregon, I attended one of their shows and stood in line next to a couple of college-age women. They had heard of OTR and a friend had invited them, but they had not actually heard the group. They were discussing the group and asked another person in line what kind of instruments they used. "None" was the response, to which one of the young women looked at the other in amazement and said "but what do they do?" They sing, and singing is not called the "first art" for nothing.

One of my former co-workers, who is retired and lives her musical life mainly within the classical and operatic tradition, attends many OTR and Divisi shows. Her favorite song in their repertoire is "Romeo and Juliet," with Jeremy Davidson's supple, down-home baritone solo, available on OTR's first CD. After she had been to a couple of their shows and was singing the song in the hallway, I asked her what she thought of the Dire Straits original, which is a favorite of mine. She looked at me and said:

"Who is Dire Straits?"

Yes, modern American song is different from that of Rorem's generation, but it is in good hands.

May 8, 2007
Reginald to Alan

Hey Alan,

It's getting rather late and I need to go to bed soon, especially as I've had a very stressful and upsetting day. (At least there's been no further sign of the rodent.) But, as I type while listening to Aqualung (a very good British singer-songwriter I've just discovered, who's given himself a ridiculous name), I am reminded by your message of conversations Robert and I have had about the fact that today (the 2000s) families have much less splintered musical lives than they did. Boomer and younger parents haven't stopped listening to popular music as used to be the case, say with the transition to adulthood in the 1940s and the 1950s, when one part of growing up was that you stopped listening to rock'n'roll or pop music, and largely stopped listening to music at all. Boomer and younger parents are not only still listening to the music they listened to in their youth, but are often also listening to the music their kids listen to, which these days is largely a pastiche of older musical styles, especially Eighties music.

Even a lot of the "new" music sounds pretty familiar to young parents, and a lot of kids listen to the music their parents listened to, from the Rolling Stones and the Doors to Led Zeppelin to Madonna and Culture Club. So I actually think that at the moment there's less of a musical generation gap than there may ever have been, at least since the era of recorded and broadcast popular music.

Just a few thoughts before bed. I will show Robert your piece. His email, by the way, is [deleted]. He's not checking it so often now that the semester is over and for the first time he doesn't have to teach during the summer (he got a much-deserved research grant from his school).

By the way, I really would love to come read at the U of Oregon if it can be managed. I really appreciate your thinking of me.

Have a great night.

peace and poetry, Reginald

May 8, 2007
Alan to Reginald

Enjoyed your recent posts. I am often intensely inspired by a particular piece of music to the point that I play it many times over in order to get it completely inside of me, where it can serve as a sort of charged battery of inspiration to be drawn on as needed. I have lately played the second movement of Colin Brumby's Symphony No. 1 maybe 50 times in four months since the composer (an Australian) sent it to me.

I am slowly pecking away at a novel and that ten minutes of music provides a perfect aquifer to feed a particular section of the story: it flows at exactly the right speed in precisely the right direction with matching dynamics. That sounds crazy but it works.

Hope you are feeling better and that the r-*-t has been dealt with.

Alan

May 8, 2007
Reginald to Alan

Dear Alan:

I too often listen to a favorite piece of music, classical or artpop, to inspire myself to write. I love your image of listening to music to charge the battery of inspiration. I really am going to bed now. Good night.

Reginald

Reginald Shepherd
On George Barker

While George Barker was quite popular in Great Britain during the 1930s and 1940s, he seems to be better remembered for his numerous love affairs and fifteen children by several different women than for his very large body of poetry. One of these affairs is chronicled in the 1945 autobiographical novel *By Grand Central Station I Sat Down and Wept* by Elizabeth Smart, a Canadian writer with whom Barker had a protracted and tumultuous relationship involving a great deal of deceit on his part and a great deal of credulity on hers. Barker's version of the affair can be found in his 1950 novel *The Dead Seagull*. As I have often written, neither the meaning nor the value of a writer's work is determined by his or her biography, but Barker's life is a fascinating read in itself. He was the very definition of the modern bohemian, who built a life around flouting social and sexual mores.

From what I can tell, Barker was never much read in America. Despite his early success as a poet, in Britain he was somewhat overshadowed in the 1940s by the Auden circle's discursive, socially oriented verse, and was rather dismissed in the 1950s by the Movement, which, reacting against what it saw as the Romantic excesses of the Forties, sought a sober, prosaic (even when written in traditional forms), "realistic" decorum to which Barker's poetry is the antithesis.

Yeats included Barker in his highly idiosyncratic *Oxford Anthology of Modern Verse 1892-1935*, in which he called him a forerunner of a future literary revolution. Philip Larkin (a leading figure in the Movement) also included Barker in his only slightly less idiosyncratic *Oxford Anthology of Twentieth-Century English Verse* (1973). But Barker's work is not included in any of the three editions of *The Norton Anthology of Modern* Poetry, nor in the recent Oxford *Anthology of Twentieth-Century British and Irish Poetry*, edited by Keith Tuma, which takes as one of its aims the restoration of forgotten or neglected poets to public attention. His absence from the latter is especially notable, since such contemporaries working in comparable exploratory modes as Dylan Thomas, the English Surrealist David Gascoyne, Nicholas Moore (founder of the New Apocalypse movement), and W.S. Graham are included.

George Granville Barker was born in 1913 and died in 1991. Barker came from a poor background in a period of intense class-consciousness and class stratification; he was largely self-educated; having left school at fourteen and worked at a variety of jobs before finding literary patronage and early success as a poet. His first "official" volume, *Poems*, was published in 1935 by Faber and Faber under the aegis of T.S. Eliot, who became Barker's patron, literary and financial, though Eliot considered him "a very peculiar fellow."

Barker's poetry, like that of Dylan Thomas and the somewhat younger W.S. Graham, is dense, musical, highly lyrical, romantic, visionary, and frequently mingles mysticism and sexuality. All three have been characterized as both New Romantic and New Apocalypse poets, though Barker and Thomas were more influences on than members of those movements. Their work certainly is romantic with both a small and a capital "R," and apocalyptic in the original sense of the Latin and Greek words "to uncover" or "to reveal." Strongly sound-led, Barker's work eschews or leaps over linear logic in favor of the logic of associations, imagistic, verbal (he's very fond of puns), and musical. "I now no longer wander wondering who."

Barker's highly dramatic work can be overly rhetorical, even oratorical, and his diction and phrasing, while usually surprising yet apt, can sometimes be slightly archaic or overly "poetic." He was highly prolific, and does not seem to have edited himself much. But his work is never complacent, never content with what has already been done; his was a restless and exploratory sensibility. Even when he writes in traditional forms like the sestina, the sonnet, and the ballad, there is in Barker's poetry an excess and a disregard for literary propriety very rare in British poetry. His best work (which to my mind is mostly found in his earlier books) has a passion and intensity that is almost overwhelming. Barker's is a unique and idiosyncratic voice that deserves to be heard again. In its verbal and emotional extravagance and even recklessness, the American poet whose work his most resembles is his near-contemporary Robert Duncan.

The most recent edition of Barker's *Collected Poems*, a volume of over eight hundred pages edited by Robert Fraser, was published by Faber and Faber in 1987, but now seems to be out of print. Fraser's substantial biography, *The Chameleon Poet: A Life of George Barker*, also appears to be out of print. Perhaps this is appropriate, as Barker was convinced that his biography couldn't be written: "I've stirred the facts around too much. It simply can't be done."

The poems in this selection are taken from Barker's *Collected Poems 1930 to 1965*, published by October House (New York) in 1965. I present them in chronological order. I have been unable to reproduce the indentations in "Daedalus."

Daedalus

I

Like the enormous liner of his limbs
and fell.
Remain behind, look on
What's left of what was once in blighted remains.
That imponderable body
Smote my desire, now smitten
Mortally.
I lift his head, his death dampens
The moist palm of my hand like handled fear
Like fear cramping my hand
and stand.
Remain behind, entertain posthumous fear.

II

Come where no crowds can trouble us divert us
No acrobats hawkers bottles or street musicians
No towering necks like buildings overlook
Intimate revelation.

I take your hand
Spectre
And steadily lead you
Across morning haunted lawns in earlier
Days, and show
With a reversal of our growing older
How it began, what caused, the germ of time.

Where florid in the night pregnant nightdresses
Proceed sedately down unlighted stairs
Like people. And in the garden
Large lake unreal. Hark, I hear visitant
Swans, and the moths in the trees
Like minor caverns humming. There he draws
Antennae from paralyzed spiders, weapons
In his warlock fingers brandished: or runs
Engendering the eventual major strength like engines
Preparant. I cannot discern you in the leaves or in the
Undergrowth, when starting down the steep hills
He flies precipitate: Spectre, Spectre, where
If among these early places lie you, do you lie?

He fell, not then. Recently sure has fallen from that high
Platform. Formed in fearlessness, has fallen
Like through thought's clouds through fear, as You stood
Waiting with wanting breast to catch, he in his fall
Evaded. Passed towards a grave straight through.
Of Course You Knew, for saw his comet face
Approaching downward like irresistible.
I mourn him. Him I mourn, from morn to morning.

III

Where once he trod
I cannot tread;
From the home he is gone from
I am prohibited:
We cannot be
While he is gone from being;
While he is not with being
I am as well miserably unloving;
Totally bereft I too am totally absent,
Appearing here, although
Bruisable and buriable seeming, am too bruised
In my dead
To buried.
Spectre who spreads
Internal dissension,

45

Dividing the unit army of the body
To coward forces,
Since I have brought
To these private places
Sick with his not being, with his recalled
Reverberant fleet blooms of doing and coming,
Empty with his going, since accomplished, entertained,
Shown choicest hothouse blossoms, phenomenal
Plants he acted on the air like dances lasting,
Since he is not here but where you know with doom—

IV

Where wander those once known herons
Or rabbits here
With shattered entrapped forepaws pitiable in crimson
Killing have known,
And seven-year-old boys locked among ominous
Shadows, enveloped
Have known, and are
At the unmerciful onrush of determined seas
Gathers small craft
There the acquainted faces of the dead sailors
Sight that sees
Where those once known herons fled in fear, to where I
Like lonely herons
The abandoned heroine

V

Go. With mild gradual descent
Burden the memory
Not as he fell, in anger, in the combat
With forms invisible intactual fought
On that mortal rooftop: not with celestial
Speed brought down, in meritorious
Defeat no beating, but like lamed
Herons or birds in wounded slope
Descending down to lamentable homes
In scraggy caves, borne down by death, I come
Drawn down to earth, and underneath

The earth, like one drawn under
Lethal water by an unknown weight
Unseen invisible, but not unknown is fear.

Narcissus

My tired lips received that morning
Their first kiss, so stirred the mind
Cannot subside for days for weeks or months.
That slim mouth upon mine held firm complete pressure,
Keeping mine for the inconceivable period
Between meeting in dream and meeting the unknown person.

Therefore for days or months I examined all faces
That slip between me and the exit to forget;
At political meetings at parties and at festivals
Every unrecognizing face, the features of every unrecognized
face, refused
To be that face, assumed adverse reaction,
Closed its cold eyes on the air, and was removed.

Traveling through a fine evening in a car
The attentive line of my own face was at intervals caught
From the sunlight in outline—the chin's framed curve,
Lips, jaw's asseveration—on the windscreen;
The reproduction on, the reality through
I now no longer wander wondering who.

"O Who Will Speak from a Womb or a Cloud?"

Not less light shall the gold and the green lie
On the cyclonic curl and diamonded eye, than
Love lay yesterday on the breast like a beast.
Not less light shall God tread my maze of nerve
Than that great dread of tomorrow drove over
My maze of days. Not less terrible that tread
Stomping upon your grave than I shall tread there.
Who is a god to haunt the tomb but Love?

Therefore I shall be there at morning and midnight,
Not with a straw in my hair and a tear as Ophelia
Floating along my sorrow, but I shall come with
The cabala of things, the cipher of nature, so that
With the mere flounce of a bird's feather crest
I shall speak to you where you sit in all trees,
Where you conspire with all things that are dead.
Who is so far that Love cannot speak to him?

So that no corner can hide you, no autumn of leaves
So deeply close over you that I shall not find you,
To stretch down my hand and sting you with life
Like poison that resurrects. O remember
How once the Lyrae dazzled and how the Novembers
Smoked, so that blood burned, flashed its mica,
And that was life. Now if I dip my hand in your grave
Shall I find it bloody with autumn and bright with stars?
Who is to answer if you will not answer me?

But you are the not yet dead, so cannot answer.
Hung by a hair's breadth to the breath of a lung,
Nothing you know of the hole over which you hang
But that it's dark and deep as tomorrow midnight.
I ask, but you cannot answer except with words
Which show me the mere interior of your fear,
The reverse face of the world. But this,
This is not death, the standing on the head
So that a sky is seen. O who
Who but the not yet born can tell me of my bourne?

Lie you there, lie you there, my never, never,
Never to be delivered daughter, so wise in ways
Where you perch like a bird beyond the horizon,
Seeing but not being seen, above our being?
Then tell me, shall the meeting ever be,
When the corpse dives back through the womb
To clasp his child before it ever was?
Who but the dead can kiss the not yet born?

Sad is space between a start and a finish,
Like the rough roads of stars, fiery and mad.

I go between birth and the urn, a bright ash
Soon blazed to blank, like a fire-ball. But
Nothing I bring from the before, no message,
No clue, no key, no answer. I hear no echo,
Only the sheep's blood dripping from the gun,
The serpent's tear like fire along the branch.
O who will speak from a womb or a cloud?

To My Mother

Most near, most dear, most loved and most far,
Under the window where I often found her
Sitting as huge as Asia, seismic with laughter,
Gin and chicken helpless in her Irish hand,
Irresistible as Rabelais, but most tender for
The lame dogs and hurt birds that surround her—
She is a procession no one can follow after
But be like a little dog following a brass band.

She will not glance up at the bomber, or condescend
To drop her gin and scuttle to a cellar,
But lean on the mahogany table like a mountain
Whom only faith can move, and so I send
O all my faith, and all my love to tell her
That she will move from mourning into morning.

Turn on Your Side and Bear the Day to Me

Turn on your side and bear the day to me
Beloved, sceptre-struck, immured
In the glass wall of sleep. Slowly
Uncloud the borealis of your eye
And show your iceberg secrets, your midnight prizes
To the green-eyed world and to me. Sin
Coils upward into thin air when you awaken
And again morning announces amnesty over
The serpent-kingdomed bed. Your mother
Watched with as dove an eye the unforgivable night
Sigh backward into innocence when you

Set a bright monument in her amorous sea.
Look down, Undine, on the trident that struck
Sons from the rock of vanity. Turn in the world
Sceptre-struck, spellbound, beloved,
Turn in the world and bear the day to me.

May 16, 2007
Alan to Reginald

What an amazing sound, Barker. Sound seems the only correct word. Like standing in a wind tunnel full of words. Yowza wowza ! Another poet some of whose work feels close to this is you. There are not many poets who can harness this kind of word-storm and ride it through to the end.

Thanks for sharing this poet's work. I had never heard of him.

Alan

May 17, 2007
Reginald to Alan

Hi Alan,

I'm glad that you liked the Barker. Your image of a wind tunnel full of words is incredibly vivid and evocative—perfect for Barker. And thanks so much, again, for your kind words about my words. I'm pretty sure that just about no one has heard of Barker, which is one of the reasons I wanted to write about him. I don't do it systematically, but one of the things I want to do with the blog is bring underread writers to whatever public attention I can muster for them.

We just got DSL service, which took all day to get working properly, and I now have a new email address, though I'll still be able to check the old one via web mail. My new address is: [deleted]

Take good care.

peace and poetry, Reginald

May 17, 2007
Alan to Reginald

I'll have to fish for used copies of Barker on ABE. I just spent a vast amount of money on the bound set of complete works of John Jay Chapman[23] (an American essayist I had never heard of until recently) as a housewarming present for my new study (former garage), so it will be a while before I buy many new books ! But I can't live without books !

DSL is very nice but it will occasionally hiccup or turn itself off. I always misplace the various codes and instructions to get it back up – keep yours where you can find them.

Wolfowitz has quit, yahoooo ! One small step for man,....

May 17, 2007
Reginald to Alan

Dear Alan,

I had copies of Barker years ago, then got rid of them for reasons unknown to me, and recently bought a couple again (his first book and that 1965 *Collected Poems,* which is the volume I used to have) on ABE, which had them for much cheaper prices than Amazon's used vendors were offering. I buy too many books, and too many CDs, but almost always used, because I am poor. The problem with buying used things, of course, is that too often they're not in the advertised condition, and then I have to raise a stink to get a refund.

When I was teaching I got a lot of books as examination copies. I can still get history and social science books that way through Robert (he teaches anthropology). I just have to let him know what examination copies "he" has requested, in case a publisher's rep comes by and asks him about it.

I've heard good things about John Jay Chapman, but have never read anything of his.

After I spent all day trying to make the DSL service work, it did exactly what you said--it just turned itself off. I was about to have a breakdown. I just spent about forty minutes with a technical support person. At least he was actually able to fix the problem, which isn't always the case.

I'm glad that Wolfowitz is gone from the World Bank, but I have little faith that he'll be replaced by anyone better. And he

---

[23] *The Collected Works of John Jay Chapman,* 1970. M&S, Weston, Mass. (currently Rhode Island).

wasn't forced out for his real crimes (which are all perfectly legal), but just for giving his girlfriend some undeserved perks, which in the bigger context doesn't really matter to me.

Take good care. I need to rest for a while. Working on this DSL situation has tired me out.

peace and poetry, Reginald

June 1, 2007
Alan to Reginald

Hi Reginald. Sorry I have not corresponded lately. I was birding in eastern Oregon for a week (plenty of birds, plenty of mosquitos) and am about to leave for my long-planned birding tour with friends in Alaska. That along with moving stuff into newly remodeled space has eaten all my time.

Enjoyed your recent blogs and Robert's. I find myself examining race through the lens of birding. I have lived mostly in small cities in Oregon, with three years in central Missouri. In my forty years of birding I have met (to speak with and know) exactly two black birders, one of whom, Drew Lanham, was visiting from South Carolina (I showed him a life Marbled Murrelet), where he is now associate professor of forest ecology and the other was a teenager from Seattle, where he is the adopted son of a white mother, oddly named Sullivan but with a heavy German accent. He's still there, in his late 20s and still birding.[24] Two, in forty years.

People meet most of their friends and social companions at work or through shared interests. For that reason I don't meet many black people in Oregon (I would if I lived in Portland) although I did in Missouri. But in Missouri, with many bird clubs and events, I met no black birders at all. I know of none in Portland.

Why not? What is it about birding culture, if you will, that doesn't appeal to black people as a "class" ? I have thought at least a little bit about the question of income and economic class. I don't think that's the main explanation, because I have known plenty of whitish people who are barely middle class and

---

[24] Patrick Sullivan is now deceased.

yet manage to get binoculars and enjoy the experience. I concede that most birders are in higher education and income levels. But higher-income blacks don't seem to take up birding or, indeed, get involved in other kinds of nature work.

Do you or Robert know any black birders? I'd be very interested in your thoughts about this. There aren't a lot of Hispanics, either, but there are some – mainly imports as adults (e.g. From Chile or Mexico), not Mexican-Americans unless they are of my subspecies: two generations downstream from immigration.

Regards - Alan

PS did you get rid of the r*t ?

June 2, 2007
Reginald to Alan

Hi Alan,

Thanks for your note, and I'm glad that you've been enjoying my blog and Robert's. I'm really not a birder myself—I went with Robert quite a lot, but kind of burned out. A little nature goes a long way for me. Robert hasn't gone much in the past couple of years himself, because school has kept him so busy. I know that he'd like to do more. This summer he has a research grant and so isn't teaching for the first time, but you don't want to hang around in the woods here in the summer—the bugs will eat you alive, and keep on eating you once you've died.

I don't know anything about the racial dynamics of birding (neither of us has ever belonged to any organization), but I'm sure that they're murky and complex, like all things racial in this society. Class and race obviously are involved in the dearth of black birders, but how that mix plays out in that particular context I couldn't even begin to guess.

The r-t seems to have been a temporary sojourner (knock on wood). I read in the paper that if one suspects a rodent infestation (as in seeing a r-t crawling around in one's garage, though the article only mentioned mice), one should block up the hole with a plastic bag and check whether it's been disturbed. Robert did that and it doesn't seem to have been moved in over a week, so he is going to board up the hole in the garage ceiling. He didn't want to do that until he knew the r-t was gone, lest it die up there and stink up the joint.

Now that the DSL service has made it feasible to download music and even videos, I recently started using iTunes, which is good way to get songs without having to buy albums I don't want, but is also very temperamental. The "network connection" likes to time out while I'm trying to download something, even though my DSL connection is working fine, and today I discovered that trying to play a CD through iTunes will make my computer crash, every time. Technology is fun.

Take good care.

peace and poetry, Reginald

Reginald Shepherd
Reflections on Poetry and Disaster

It seems that everyone and then some has weighed in with his or her responses to or thoughts about the events of September 11, 2001, so I thought that I would make my contribution as well. Poetry played an important role in helping me come to grips with both those events and what was made of them in the media. As for most people in America and around the world, my only access to those events and their aftermath was through their media representation. Though I grew up there and remember the construction of the World Trade Center, I no longer live in New York City and don't know anyone who was directly affected.

William Carlos Williams famously but not, I think, accurately wrote that, though the news cannot be found in poetry, men die every day for lack of what is found there. It distorts what poetry actually offers to aggrandize it in this way. People die every day, often in large numbers, for all sorts of quite material reasons, and many people live perfectly well, even happily, without poetry. As Edna St. Vincent Millay, also famously, wrote of love, it is not meat nor drink, nor slumber nor a roof against the rain. And yet, it's much better to live with it than without it.

I do believe that poetry embodies and enacts kinds of knowledge, and not just thematically, but in its form. One kind of knowledge poetry enacts is that of rightness of relation, of part to part, of part to whole, and of whole to part. This rightness of relation is a model or an imago of a just society. Though many things in our world are an affront to the very idea of such a society, that rightness of relation was a consolation to me in responding to what has become known as 9/11.

Death, Continuance, and the Lights

A poem that I turned to in the aftermath of the destruction of the World Trade Center seems on the surface to have nothing to do with the disaster, but it nonetheless resonated very much for me. It's by Mei-mei Berssenbrugge, and appears in her first book, *Random Possession*, published in 1979 by I. Reed Books and sadly now out of print. Here is the full text of the poem.

Suspension Bridge

You say all of us
even if we fail become lights
along the awesome bones. Separated
by darkness, humming through wires
on windy nights, bellying out
you're so sure the current is personal

Not like the firefly
that lives for a month
jolted at random by a blank force
that never knows the brightness
of its shocked body
even on cool nights above the grasses
when it loves, victim to victim.

One thing that moves me about this poem is the promise of continuance, the sense of cycle in the poem's melding of the man-made with the natural world: we die as individuals but life goes on, our works fade or collapse but the work of making continues. The hint of immortality in the promise that we will all become lights makes the terribly clichéd notion of a thousand points of light concrete in the image of the world as a field of glowing fireflies (corresponding to the image of the bridge as a string of lights). Given the context of socio-political extremity, I can't help but think of the end of Auden's "September 1, 1939" (rather too obvious a choice about which to write, though I re-read it many times in the weeks following September 11), the ironic points of light of the Just flashing out their messages. I don't have Auden's confidence of being among the just, let alone the Just. The modesty of Berssenbrugge's claims feels much more appropriate to me, the tentativeness of the hope it proffers more accurate and realistic.

Though this poem is about a bridge, I think of the World Trade Center's awesome bones (the myriad vertical struts making up the structural redundancy that was intended to permit the towers to survive the impact of an airplane crashing into them), now bent and broken. "The blank force/that never knows the brightness/of its shocked body" will for me always evoke the planes crashing into those shining towers on that bright clear morning. But I am still consoled by the poem's assurance that our lights are not merely fireflies, fleeting victims flickering quickly out of existence, but will go on: that though lives end, life goes on. There are moments at which truisms are nothing less than true. Despite the apparent distance of its subject matter from the horrors of September 11 (though the poem does deal with a massive structure of human design), it's the poem's juxtaposition of death and survival, its sense of recurrence and things going on despite death, including and containing death, that makes the connection for me. And the lights.

Some Things to Do With Tears

I read Allen Grossman 's collection *How to Do Things With Tears* several times in the aftermath of the September 11, 2001 attacks and it was a source of great solace to me, a reminder of the news it is possible to get from poetry, and the life, of the spirit if not always of the body, that poetry can help sustain. The book addresses the question of what is to be done with tragedy and mortality, of how they can be addressed without being trivialized or merely turned into more poetry.

My poem "Objects in Mirror Are Closer Than They Appear," which appears in my most recent book, *Fata Morgana*, is a poem "about" the World Trade Center disaster, or at least about the mediated spectacle of the disaster (the mirror being of course the television screen through which I and most people experienced it). The poem was born under Grossman's sign, as it were. *How to Do Things With Tears*, and the notes at the end of it, especially the second note, gave me a way toward this difficult subject, as well as an admonition about the dangers of approaching it at all. And I did find myself in tears at several points watching the televised deaths of strangers in a city in which I had not lived in years. Grossman's book showed me what might be done with those useless, vicarious tears.

I used Grossman's phrase "there is nothing that will suffice," as one of the poem's original epigraphs, to underscore my sense that in such a situation poetry indeed, as Auden wrote, did nothing, and that perhaps what it did was of dubious worth, but then decided that it was perhaps too directive and explanatory of my intentions. I felt somewhat ambivalent about writing this poem, and about the impulse to write it, not wanting to make poetic capital out of suffering (in the way that the relentless media exploitation of the catastrophe made so much more literal capital out of it), but the poem is critical (and self-critical) about the impulse to turn suffering into song (what the marvelous poet Michael Anania called in a note to me elegy as felix culprit), and about the vicarious participation in the pain of others.

In one passage of his book's notes, Grossman writes that "Any NEW poetry must be aware that there is nothing that will suffice. Any new poetry must be aware of insufficiency, unanswerability in response to what anybody knows, with respect to what consciousness is conscious of. There is, in this matter of poetic thinking (poetic realism), no distinction possible to be made between consciousness and moral consciousness." I tried to get something of that sense into the poem, to have the poem itself critique poetry's relentless urge to turn the world into elegy, another occasion for song, music however mournful. My own work has tended to be much about that mournful music, so there was definitely a self-critique involved. The church sign, by the way, is real, as are the songs.

In an interview with *The Harvard Advocate*, Grossman says that "A strong poetry would be a poetry that discerns and finds a poetically adequate means of bringing to mind the catastrophe of history." "Objects in Mirror Are Closer than They Appear" was my attempt, perhaps foredoomed by definition, to find such a poetically adequate means of confronting rather than simply surrendering to history.

Objects in Mirror Are Closer Than They Appear

I stow this moment with all the other baggage
too heavy to be carried or left
behind. Roadside church sign says *The Lord*
is the Lord who made us the way we are us.
He scatters the remnants and collects
them at a later date (unspecified): sorts them
into neat piles. I have watched twin towers fall
a dozen times. An absence moves through
the wreckage while the light stays put; the rats

will have to find another home.

Song keeps repeating *I watched you suffer*
even after the song's turned off.

History picks her way in high heels
through the structural redundancy (still shimmering
with its recentness, its haze of airborne ash
and grit), compassion makes his way through the structured
inequality in blue serge suit to interview survivors of
the structural adjustment, the combined
and uneven development that bursts into flames
at half an hour intervals, implodes
in slow motion with a televisual sigh
(catches up with photogenic falling bodies).

Song wants to soothe the sidewalk misery
into grief, smooth the debris into a shroud.

Lamed truth hobbles into another dark
through crumpled girders and concrete, calibrating
ruin and song, ruining the song
for the sake of what was life: hands out these
glass splinters, mercies and atrocities
that can't be lulled into music,
the ignorance we call innocence.
They taste like burning (a violent antidote),
incapable of caring if it harmonizes, or
unwilling to succumb again.

Song won't shut up, keeps saying *Don't look
down*. Justice tries to listen for a low tapping sound.

July 6, 2007
Alan to Reginald

Enjoyed your blognote on poetry about disaster.[25] The trick is to write *from* the experience of the disaster without writing *about* the disaster so specifically that the poem ages poorly.

James Merrill once said in an interview (I scuttled across the room to find it) that a problem with writing about current events is that "when the tide of feeling goes out, the language begins to stink."[26] I have always appreciated that view and the Merrilly twist to the phrase.

Hope all is well.

Alan

July 6, 2007
Reginald to Alan

Hey Alan,

Thanks for your note, and your very smart comments. Would you mind posting them as a comment on the blog? I like the idea of making such observations part of the public conversation.

I'm okay. The rat seems to have been a temporary sojourner. Robert plugged the hole with a plastic bag (I saw that in an article in the paper) and it hasn't been disturbed. And I, in turn, am less disturbed.

Sunday is Robert's birthday. He'll be thirty-six. Did you see his post on crashing bird populations? Very depressing, and (especially combined with crashing bee populations) with scary implications for the human future. As the Checkers commercial says, you gotta eat.

Take good care. all best, Reginald

---

[25] "Reflections on Poetry and Disaster", preceding pages.

[26] James Merrill, in an interview with John Boatwright and Enrique Ucelay DaCal, in J. D. McClatchy and Stephen Yenser, eds., *Collected Prose: James Merrill*, 2004, p. 72. Knopf.

Reginald Shepherd
Ann Lauterbach on Schools, Movements, and Poetic Identities

One of the benefits of having a web log is that it puts one in contact with people one would otherwise never interact with. Conversely, one of the drawbacks of having a web log is that it puts one in contact with people one would otherwise never interact with. In some of my recent online interactions, I have been struck by the eagerness of some people to label me and make sweeping assumptions about my tastes, opinions, and positions, often on the basis of a proudly professed ignorance of anything me or my work. They simply decided that, not being a member of their club, I must be one of "Them," and thus irredeemably worthless if not outright evil. These interactions, in turn, have me thinking again about the will to categorize, label, and pigeonhole both oneself as a writer and other writers that is so prevalent in the online poetry world. Such fixations on labels and side-taking seem more prevalent in the online poetry world (certainly in the world of poetry blogs) than in the print poetry world, where things are much more fluid and flexible, though such compulsive territorializing and fence-building is far from absent there either.

Ann Lauterbach, a brilliant poet and an equally brilliant thinker about poetry, has in various essays made several acute observations on this situation, as well as its larger intellectual and social context, in which poems are defined, judged, and even written (but rarely actually read) in terms of their authors' social or ideological identities, whether presumed or professed, imposed or embraced. I quote them here for the edification of all interested parties.

> "It is no secret that the academy has, over the past several decades, increasingly stressed theoretical and critical reading, promulgating a subtle inversion by which so-called primary texts have become secondary, mere pretexts to argue or 'prove' one critical ideology or another. Much that is invigorating and compelling has come of this, providing a hugely expanded vocabulary for discussing aesthetic objects, but there are danger signs, at least in the poetic community, of an increasingly eviscerated and arid landscape. The

aspiring young poet begins to write in such a way as to invite a certain critical attention, to 'fit' her work into one or another critical category. This is the main function of being identified with a group or school, to draw critical attention that individual poets, not affiliated with a movement or group, cannot easily attract. 'New York School' or 'Language Poetry' are given brand-name status, commodifying and homogenizing, so that critics (and poets) can make general identifications and totalizing critiques without having to actually contend with the specific differences among and between so-called members of the group. Those not so identified are left out, often understandably embittered or confused, as the idea of an individual iconoclastic poet gives way to collaborative and tribal identities. Thus the marginalized world of poetry begins to imitate other identity formulations which increasingly govern contemporary academic, cultural, and political life. Frightened by exclusionary clubs, the poet ceases to identify herself with the essential margin from which a vital critique must come."

"In this culture, the choice begins to be either to move into the denuded brilliance of celebrity or become part of a group which knows itself not because its little dog knows it but because it represents the Society of Little Dogs. Thus allegiances are formed not so much by ideological choice but by a priori cultural determinates; one identifies with those who most resemble what one already claims as identification (I am a woman, therefore I must be a feminist). The idea that the act of reading expands and extends knowledge to orders of unfamiliar experience has been replaced by acts of reading in order to substantiate and authorize claims and positions which often mirror the identity bearings of the reader."

This is a wonderful Gertrude Stein quote that Lauterbach cites: "The manner and habits of Bible times or Greek or Chinese have nothing to do with ours today but the masterpieces exist just the same and they do not exist because of their identity, that is what any one remembering then remembered then, they do not exist by human nature because everybody always knows everything there is to know about human nature, they exist because they come to be as something that is an end in itself and in that respect is opposed to the business of living which is relation and necessity" (Gertrude Stein, "What Are Master-pieces and Why Are There So Few of Them?"). "Misquotations from Reality," *Diacritics*, 26:3-4, Fall/Winter 1996. pp. 152, 153.

"Among my graduate writing students there was a noticeable deficit of references to sources, literary or otherwise, outside their immediate foreground; among African-American students, I found a tendency to write from the perspective of racial identity that demanded a public stance toward the self, as if the self were a stereotypical example whose voice must uphold, and reflect, the most unnuanced and prolific negative assumptions about black life in America. Individuailty was conflated with identity...."

"The Night Sky II," *The Night Sky: Writings on the Poetics of Experience.* New York: Viking, 2005, p. 77.

"[W]e need to question the notion that we can talk with any clarity about the academy when there are so many institutions that now invest in contemporary writing, each of which has a different perspective on, and alignment to, poetic lineage and practice. These perspectives are often directly attributable to the specific poetics of poet/teachers within a given program....

"We need to think about how so-called 'schools' come into being, through what agencies they disseminate and become part of an historical narrative. I am thinking, for instance, of the poet in and around Black Mountain, the New York School, the Beats, the San Francisco Renaissance, the Harlem Renaissance, and L=A=N=G=U=A=G=E, each of which represents a particular extension and hybridization of a recognizable poetics. At what point does a group of poets with a loose configuration of affinities and concerns become a school or movement, and at what point does this named entity become the property of literary history, a commodity?" [RS: I question in what way a literary movement, however reified, can become a commodity in any but the loosest metaphorical sense.]

"The Night Sky IV," *op. cit.*, p. 102, 103.

Alan Contreras said...

A literary movement can become a commodity, or at least a brand, to the extent that what its members produce is purchased by a definable group of people. In the case of poetry production, that group may well be each other, within or hovering on the fringes of that movement.

But what a horrible idea, "poetry production." I suppose in today's literary climate in which being a successful poet means being employed primarily because one is a poet—that is, paid to be an academic poet instead of having an ordinary life and writing from that experience—it's a natural term.

As for writing from a group identity rather than an individual identity, doing so generates a certain level of safety, protection, and what I am fond of calling an uncompromising commitment to adequacy. This is hivewriting: the hum is constant and the result a good nap.

What it never does is produce excellence. However, in that it matches our American society. We live in an age that is threatened by excellence, resists it, especially in education, and thinks any kind of clear statement of position contrary to the way the bulls are running is socially damaging (to the speaker) and unprofessional.

The great American essayist John Jay Chapman, who always knew bull on sight and which way it was running, wrote of the "general cowardice" of the age (this in 1900) and recommended a dose of truth thus:

"Everybody in America is soft, and hates conflict. The cure for this, both in politics and social life, is the same, hardihood. Give them raw truth. They think they will die. ... The whole problem...is to get people to stop simpering and

65

saying "After You" to cant."[27]

Chapman was writing mainly of how people interact in society and government, but the same problem—and the same solution—applies in the fine arts. An astonishing number of poetry's royalty are parading about unclothed but for their crowns. Let us say so instead of mounting up behind them.

Reginald Shepherd said...

Dear Alan,

I'm not sure that a literary community can be a commodity, but I definitely see how it can become a brand, marketing a trademark style to an audience expecting a certain kind of poetic "product." Obviously this phenomenon occurs with both "mainstream" poets and with "avant-garde" poets. Critic Vernon Shetley has written in the Irish journal *Metre* of "a poetry world where each poet seems compelled to enhance his or her brand recognition with an easily recognizable gimmick."

---

[27] John Jay Chapman, *Practical Agitation*, 1900, revised ed. 1909, p. 49. Moffat, Yard. Reprinted in Melvin Bernstein, ed., *Collected Works of John Jay Chapman*, Vol. 2, 1970. M&S, Providence, RI.

Alan Contreras
I'm an Expert (or how I lenskafied myself)

I am an expert. Everyone tells me so. They tell me that I am an expert on diploma mills and degree fraud because I have been working professionally in that field for many years. I have become either glorious or notorious, depending on whether the person evaluating me got a degree from a genuine college. I am invited to write book chapters and introductions and give speeches and testimony, owing to my general splendor in that arena. However, I don't have any degrees in higher-education administration or policy.

They tell me that I am an expert on birds because I have published three books about them, including co-editing Birds of Oregon (Oregon State University Press, 2003), a five-pounder whose bibliography contains 4,000 citations. I proved that volume's worth and my expertise when asked, by a person who hadn't seen it, if she could carry it in her pocket in the field. I said, "Sure, if you're a large kangaroo or a small aircraft." I don't have any degrees in ornithology, either.

I may be a nascent expert in a few other subjects - time will tell. Or will it? Who makes those decisions, anyway?

To pick an example that may be unfairly obvious, who decided that Noam Chomsky was an expert in everything? Did he simply declare that one day, following which the assembled masses bowed down in unison? How does a renowned professor of linguistics transmute into an expert on world affairs and the human condition? Surely this is a mega-meme of great cultural import: Word has gone forth that Chomsky is an expert.

I can understand that a chemist would be treated as an expert in chemistry, and an architect an expert in design. That approach doesn't quite work, however, when novelists are classified as experts in literature for academic purposes - given that the creative force and the explicative force are profoundly different - and linguists become experts in political sociology.

The relevant difference may be between fields in which clear questions lead to definitive answers, and those in which opinions - that is, individual aesthetic or value judgments - render all truths flexible. The line may be between the sciences and everything else, or it may lie somewhere in the murk.

67

Chomsky seems to be an expert because he says he is, and enough people agree. It doesn't seem to matter which people, as long as there are enough of them. Writers such as Wendell Berry and Camille Paglia (both favorites of mine) are in a similar category.

Perhaps that is all that is necessary: We can all be the Rula Lenskas of our own domain. Do you recall the late 1970s TV ads featuring a woman who sailed forth - draped in couth, untrammeled by care, her nose in the air – and imperiously announced, "I'm Rula Lenska"? Nobody in the United States had ever heard of her, but her brazen self-declaration of splendor levitated her briefly to the status of cultural icon. In fact, she was and still is a successful if rather offbeat actress in her native Britain, and the cultural joke may be on us: She is technically a Polish countess, though not, as it were, practicing just now.

Can I, if you will, lenskafy myself? To a certain extent, I can; that is how some people develop reputations.

There are limits, of course. I could stroll into Fermilab and declare myself an expert on particle physics, and my friends George Gollin and Heidi Schellman, who really are such, would just look at me oddly, say "whatever," and go about their business. That is because I cannot really navigate the quark jungle. At some point, the waiter brings the check, and the lenskafier has to be able to pay up with appropriate coin.

However, if I declare myself an expert on, say, the poetry of Loren Eiseley, the music of Colin Brumby, or the essays of John Jay Chapman, I cannot be dismissed out of hand. I should at least have an opportunity to demonstrate my expertise. In the fine arts and many of the social sciences, there are no mazes of facts to negotiate, as there would be were I to attempt to feel my way through the glutinous slurry of quarks, leptons, and forces with which physicists work.

In theory, I can be just as much of an expert in more-subjective fields as anyone else. If I say that Brumby's Symphony No. 1 is better music than anything by Virgil Thomson and merits standing alongside the works of Edward Elgar and Samuel Barber, or that Edwin Muir is a better literary critic than Edmund Wilson, I can be challenged but not corrected. Those are judgments of value and quality.

Of course, I might end up like Wilson's fictional Galapagos iguana, which, when questioned by a fictional zoologist, declared that it knew all it needed to of its world, and that it was an über-being. Experts greater than I may pick me up by the tail and carry me off for further study, which is what happened to the iguana in Wilson's tale.

To what extent is being an expert the result of our education and the degrees we hold? My degrees from the University of Oregon are in political science and law. Neither has any special relationship to the arcana of evaluating degree programs, or anything whatsoever to do with the distribution and movements of the spotted towhee.

Alex Walker, one of the more important ornithologists in Oregon history, had a day job at a cheese factory. As far as I know, he had no college degrees at all. Was he not an expert? I met him in 1969, and he certainly seemed like one to me. His data were collected in an appropriate manner, and his articles appeared in the field's major journals.

On the other hand, we now have scores of M.F.A. factories in the United States, pumping out certified experts in poetry, fiction, drama, and that useful catch-all, literary nonfiction. Yet when we look at our best living poets - let me herewith declare that they are W.S. Merwin and Adrienne Rich - we see no such "professional" degrees. Nor do we see those degrees in most foreign countries. Even worse, some American universities now offer creative-writing Ph.D. programs, which will not give us better writers but merely add an invisible layer of academic dignity to the emperor's current unnecessary garments.

American universities also produce in great numbers that peculiar cultural artifact, the Ed.D., which seems to denote a certified education bureaucrat. Surely we need education bureaucrats in moderation - I am one, and I argue for both need and moderation from personal experience - but we don't need a unique credential for them.

Why do Americans insist on believing that degrees confer worth and qualification? The citizens of other nations are following our example here, as shown in Ronald Dore's excellent *The Diploma Disease,* but we are clearly the masters.

I have always appreciated Paul Valéry's view:

"Let us confess: The real object of education is the diploma. I never hesitate to declare that the diploma is the deadly enemy of culture. As diplomas have become more important in our lives (and their importance has done nothing but grow as a result of economic conditions), the less has education had any real effect.

... The aim of education being no longer the development of the mind but the acquisition of the diploma, the required minimum becomes the goal of study."[28]

Not long ago, I had a submission rejected (by a newspaper editor who has accepted other work of mine) on the ground that I was not enough of an expert on the subject. His concern, at least officially, was not that the piece was wrong or poorly written; it was that if he accepted my commentary as a nonexpert, he'd have to accept lots of other commentaries by nonexperts, and then where would we be?

He had rejected my attempt to lenskafy myself. Of course, he doesn't have to accept anything he doesn't want to, and it may be that he was sparing us both by not saying that he thought my piece really stank.

I hear the carping already. You object that "lenskafy" is not a real word, and that I have therefore constructed my argument on at least one faulty tower. I disagree. If Richard Dawkins, a nonlinguist, can establish the word "meme" no great number of years back, and I get to use it in this essay, then I, with equivalent professional authority, can create the word "lenskafy" and establish its meaning. I declare myself competent to so expand the English language.

I will even ask an expert linguist to weigh in on my right to do so. Noam Chomsky, where are you when I need you?

---

[28] Paul Valery, *The Outlook for Intelligence*, p. 149. Bollingen/Princeton, 1962.

July 8, 2007
Alan to Reginald

I commented on your Lauterbach post. I'll have to dig up her book.

Cheers - A

July 18, 2007
Reginald to Alan

Hi Alan,

I quite liked your recent column in *The Chronicle of Higher Education* on the problematization of knowledge and expertise. It was very witty and also very insightful. There was another article on that recently in the *Chronicle*, about how the Web has undermined intellectual authority. But in general kids today (I am so old) have a kind of contempt for the idea that anyone might know something they don't. About ten years ago a student in one of my classes said, in class, "You act like you know more than everyone else in the room," which I thought showed a remarkable lack of understanding of the basics of the pedagogical situation. I told her that I did indeed know more, about poetry anyway, than everyone in the room put together, and that she would have cause to complain if I didn't.

I was pleased to see you praise Merwin, who is a kind of eminence grise but not much read these days. I did a post about *The Lice*,[29] which I think an amazing book, a few months ago.

I did think, though, that you were too hard on creative writing programs. They're a popular and all too easy target, and while they certainly have problems, they're hardly responsible for the degradation of discourse or even of writing standards in this country. To the extent that they're part of that (which I think is exaggerated), they're only a symptom of a much larger cultural problem.

---

[29] W.S. Merwin, *The Lice*, 1967.

David Yezzi is sometimes smart, but, like most of The *New Criterion* crowd, he's much too self-conscious and self-satisfied a curmudgeon, and his aesthetic and intellectual horizons are much too narrow (perhaps deliberately, but it's no better for that). His anthology of newer poets is full of minor formalists whose only virtue is that they can (most of them, sort of) scan, which is good but hardly good enough. It's remarkable to me how many so-called New Formalists (Dana Gioia, for one) cannot scan to save their lives.

It's getting late and I should prepare for bed, but I've been meaning to write you for a while, and why put off until tomorrow what you can do today? Unless, of course, you just don't feel like it.

peace out to the homebodies and the homosexuals,

Reginald

July 19, 2007
Alan to Reginald

I'm glad you like my "expert" piece, which was a lot of fun to do. I think your response to the student is exactly right: hey you little snot, you're PAYING me because I'm supposed to have knowledge to impart to you, not so we can all go on a shared-values picnic (slap, slap).

It is hard to know exactly how to approach MFA programs. I do think that there are too many of them, preying on students' mistaken belief that they can become "professional" poets. However, having access to good writers like yourself is hard to achieve any other way (I am very glad to see you taking private students). Certainly our society allows few other places where poets can, if you will, take shelter for a while and concentrate on their work.

The Lice is indeed great. My favorite is probably *The Vixen*.[30] His poetic style is so well suited to old places, old walls, old winds, old flames. Merwin, the poet of mystic recollection.

---

[30] W. S. Merwin, *The Vixen*, 1995. Knopf.

I picked up a copy of Lauterbach's *Night Sky* book[31] (my local bookstore tells me it is OP so I had to order it off ABE) and have started into it. It's hard to "read" because it is so unlinear, but there are chunks of pure gold within the swirling flow. Her command of language leaves me creeping along in the ditch, hoping to grasp enough words as they are tossed from her passing coach.

Did I ever send you any Colin Brumby music? I have his permission to share it with friends.

I'll talk to the UO people about your glorious visit when they are findable in August.

Homotextually yours, Alan

Alan to Reginald
July 19, 2007

Hey dude, I sent the formal request and offer of swag to Karen Ford, head of UO Creative Writing, today. Will keep you posted. If she doesn't like it, I have means of persuasion....

July 19, 2007
Reginald to Alan

Dude. Thanks for putting in a plug for me to come out to UO for a reading. It would definitely be cool to get to go out there, and of course to meet you. The swag would be nice too. I never get to swagger these days...

peace, poetry, and persuasion, Reginald

July 19, 2007
Alan to Reginald

With luck the swagman cometh. Actually the swagman arriveth a while back, it is the po-queen at whose feet I casteth

---

[31] Ann Lauterbach, *The Night Sky: writings on the poetics of experience*, 2005. Viking.

my coin of the realm, no, wait, that's Carl Phillips's book, you're the OTHER living urbane black gay poet, where IS my form chart of these things, anyway? Gotta keep 'em straight. Well, aligned, anyway.

Did I ever ask you if you have read any Essex Hemphill? He's dead just now but I came across a collection of his.[32] Wow.

July 19, 2007
Reginald to Alan

Please, please, please don't confuse me with Carlo Phillipo. I have enough reminders that there's only room for one black gay classically inclined poet, and that he's the one. He's also been a pretty serious beyotch to me for many, many years.

And my forthcoming book of essays is WAY better than *Coin of the Realm*.[33]

I've read some Essex Hemphill, long ago. I was not so impressed. But I did meet him (and even go out dancing with him) when I was an MFA student at Brown. He was a very nice guy. I was sad that he died.

peace out to the homebodies and the homosexuals,

Me

July 25, 2007
Alan to Reginald

Your e-mail hasn't been working lately.

I promise NEVER to confuse you with That Other Poet. Your writing certainly can't be confused.

UO Creative Writing program would be very happy to have you come talk to their little animals. Current director is Karen Ford. They can set up an evening reading and a Friday classroom discussion time with the 36 undergrads who are in what's called the Kidd tutorial - in effect their best students. We can probably

---

[32] Essex Hemphill, *Ceremonies*, 1992. Penguin.
[33] Carl Phillips, *Coin of the Realm*, 2004. Graywolf.

add an additional informal kiss-the-poet session sometime. I'll see if I can get a local bookstore to have your books available.

I think spring would be best, maybe early April, if that works for you. There are always lots of poetry things in April so if you'd rather avoid that month we can pick another. We need to avoid the last two weeks of March (finals and break) for sure, and I won't have any money available until maybe December. Thus if you don't like April I'd be tempted to aim for late Feb or very early March.

They don't have any money so I'll pay for what is needed and hit up a couple of people I know who can't run fast enough. Can you send me an estimate of your airfare and speaking fee? I can figure out lodging here. I'm thinking about having you arrive Wednesday (it will take all day from Florida), do an open event Thursday evening, the classroom event Friday, have Saturday as a free day if desired and fly home Sunday. That also gets you (us) a better airfare. Any additional events would be tucked in somewhere.

Best one-hop air to Eugene (assuming that you can fly far west from Pensacola) is probably United via Denver (ok in April, more risky in midwinter) or Delta via Salt Lake. Or go longer-haul to Portland, Seattle or San Francisco and shuttle to Eugene.

No big hurry in planning this but it looks feasible.

Alan

July 25, 2007
Reginald to Alan

Hey Alan,

Thanks for your note. Are you sure you've been entering the right email address? I've been getting and receiving email without any problem, and even went to the webmail sites of my previous address and my current address to see if anything hasn't been coming through.

I don't like Carl Phillips as a person (I've tried over the years, but he's always been quite nasty to me), but he's written some wonderful poems. *In the Blood, After the Devotions,* and *Riding Westwards* are wonderful books, and *Cortege* is very good. I do feel that he's descended into stiff mannerism in recent years, and *The Rest of Love*[34] (which was a finalist for the National Book Award) was one of the worst books of poetry I've ever read, sentimental, platitudinous, and full of archaisms. He doesn't seem to be able to distinguish between his stronger and his weaker work, and neither does anyone else, at least the prize-nominating and - awarding anyones.

Thanks so much for wrangling this invitation to read at UO. I really appreciate it. Spring is fine with me, better than earlier in the year—I'd like to avoid weather related delays and cancellations as much as possible.

I will look up some airfares on Expedia and Travelocity and get back to you. Does that mean that you want me to buy the ticket and then get reimbursed? Just me know if that's the case, so I can work it into my financial planning (I don't have much cash flow). Thanks also for realizing that it take[s] a long time to get from here to pretty much anywhere—most people don't. I will have to go to a hub and then change planes at least once; to Eugene, which is pretty small, I might have to do it twice. I'd like to avoid United (and US Air), as they have the worst on-time arrival record of any US airline. Since there aren't many flights to Pensacola from anywhere, if a flight is delayed or cancelled (as it was when I was coming home from the low-residency MFA in program in California last month), it's very easy for me to get stuck somewhere.

My usual fee for a reading alone is $750. The last time I did a reading and a talk, I got $1000. If this is too much, I am flexible. But I'm a good reader and a good talker—you'll get your money's worth. I hope that you can line up some cute boys to kiss the poet. :-)

I also wanted to thank you for your very articulate comment on my Ann Lauterbach post.[35] I meant to respond, but I was feeling very depressed and overwhelmed for a while, and since I got out of it I've been swamped catching up on all the things I didn't do while I was in the slough of despond, like responding to the first set of packets from my California correspondence students. I like *The Night Sky*, but the essays are rather disjointed;

---

[34] Carl Phillips, *In the Blood*, 1992, Northeastern; *From the Devotions* (Reginald mis-remembered the title), 1998, Graywolf; *Riding Westwards*, 2006, Farrar Straus Giroux; *Cortege*, 1995, Graywolf; *The Rest of Love*, 2004, Farrar, Straus, Giroux.

[35] See comment at end of Lauterbach post.

sometimes I wonder what makes them essays. As you wrote, though, there are a lot of gems to be mined. And I thought that Evan Eisenberg poetry quiz[36] you sent me was quite funny. I've read *The Recording Angel* (and hadn't known there was a second edition, which I will have to look up); I have *The Ecology of Eden*[37] but haven't read it yet.

Take good care, and thanks again for setting up this reading invitation. It's amazing to me the interesting people I've gotten to know, like you, and the opportunities that have opened up because of my blog, which I started by accident. I was intending to leave a comment on Ron Silliman's blog (which I no longer read, because it and especially the rabid attack dogs in his comments section upset me) and it took me to a page to set up my own blog instead. So that comment became my first blog post.

peace and poetry, Reginald

---

[36] See following page.
[37] Evan Eisenberg, *The Recording Angel* 1988, Penguin; *The Ecology of Eden,* 1998. Knopf.

Poetic License Exam

By EVAN EISENBERG

According to Code, spaces between stanzas must be
    no greater than two inches
    no less than one yawp
    provided with a vermin-proof cap
    filled with fine sand

Which tool should be used to disassemble a Petrarchan sonnet?
    5-inch vise grip
    31/2-inch strap wrench
    Yale deconstructor
    New Criticism

To prevent leakage, the lower end of a stanza of ottava rima (e.g.
Byron's "Don Juan") should be sealed with
    a couplet
    a doublet
    a stainless-steel cap and rubber gasket sleeve
    duct tape

Enjambment is permitted when
    space does not allow installation of a fixture on one line
    a long-sweep 1/4 bend is used to connect the lines
    a relief yoke vent is installed to vent overflow
    a variance is granted by the Prosody Department

Which of the following should be used when a limited number
of words are available?
    single sanitary tee
    double sanitary tee
    3/4-inch copper sestina
    limerick

According to Code, internal rhyme may not be used unless
    it is installed at least six inches below grade
    assonance is limited by local ordinance
    metrical fittings are clearly labeled
    a schematic is filed in the building superintendent's office

Which of the following types of rhymes or rhyme schemes does not meet Code?
  macaronic
  Hudibrastic
  ABCB
  PVC

To couple a line of iambic trimeter to a line of dactylic hexameter, the poet should use a
  spondee
  trochee
  flange, gasket, and locknut
  anapest, amphibrach, and 5/8-inch compression fitting

When essential components have been installed in an open-trench quatrain, any remaining space should be filled in with
  extended metaphor
  concrete poetry
  reasonably clean backfill
  hot air

The purpose of the trap in a canto drain line is to
  hold water
  form a barrier to sewer gases
  insulate individual talent from the Tradition
  prevent afflatus from escaping into the living area

If a tanka overflows, the poet should
  relieve stress on weak syllables
  replace it with two haiku joined by a 3/4-inch street elbow
  check the cleanout for obstructions such as pleonasm or proslepsis
  use a plunger

Evan Eisenberg is an author in New York City. His books include *The Ecology of Eden* (Alfred A. Knopf, 1998) and *The Recording Angel* (second edition, Yale University Press, 2005). http://chronicle.com Section: *The Chronicle Review* Volume 53, Issue 47, Page B5, July 27, 2007. Reprinted courtesy of the author.

July 25, 2007
Alan to Reginald

I finished *The Night Sky*. A strange mix, to be sure, but I flagged a number of pages where glowing lights remain. I also recently bought a used copy of Vernon Shetley's *After the Death of Poetry*.[38] I am not a very literary person, let alone classically trained, but I gain a bit from these writers.

My hope is to simply donate all the money to the UO foundation, have it moved over to creative writing and have them do the work. If that doesn't work I'll just mail you a check as soon as you have to pay. I'll have the swag in hand by December or so, which should be plenty of time. In theory any payment you make should be covered in a week or so. Fee is fine assuming that all goes well.

Tell me what kind of boys you like and I'll see what kind of kissers I can arrange ! Yowza ! My guess is that your best route with the most options will be Delta via Atlanta, changing in Salt Lake.

Phillips has either stopped paying attention or has become enamored of his own legend. Really too bad. Some of his work is sublime.

I am toying with a blog idea of my own and have set up the shell. Not sure yet whether it is the right way to spend my time. Sold essays to Chron of Higher Ed and Inside Higher Ed this week, and there is something to be said for working on things that generate revenue.

Alan

July 26, 2007
Reginald to Alan

Hey Alan,

For a non-literary person, you have a lot more literary smarts than many self-proclaimed (and self-assured) litterateurs I

---

[38] Vernon Shetley, *After the Death of Poetry: Poet and Audience in Contemporary America*, 1993. Duke.

know and know of. I think that *After the Death of Poetry* is a very smart book. I don't necessarily agree with his choices of poets he thinks are interesting, but his thesis, that contemporary mainstream poetry is too easy, not too hard, and insufficiently intellectually engaging, is an engaging one, and he argues well for it. I drew on it for my post on difficulty in poetry.

I think that Carl was enamored of his own legend long before he had one. It is a shame, because at his best his work is marvelous and unique.

Again, I really appreciate your setting up this visit to UO. Thou swell, as the old song goes.

I have found my blog useful in numerous ways--in bringing me into contact with interesting people (again, like you) I otherwise would not have known or even known about, in raising my profile (I've gotten some publishing invitations because of it), and even in getting me work (not just the private correspondence students, but a visiting position in a low-residency MFA came my way because of the blog). And I think of most things I write for it as drafts toward a second book of literary essays. I certainly don't consider their appearance online to be publication, and I don't believe in wasting anything I write. But if people are willing to pay you for your opinions, by all means go with that instead. I suppose in part it depends on what sorts of things you'd want to write, and whether they would fall within the realm of your paying assignments.

I need to get ready to go to dinner—I've a hankering for sushi—and so will sign off now.

Take good care, and thanks again.

peace and poetry, Reginald

July 26, 2007
Alan to Reginald

I bought "Death Of" because you mentioned it and because I like James Merrill's work and am interested in what he says of

81

Merrill. I have heard Merrill called a poet of surfaces,[39] which is true in some of his work, but there is more to it than that.

Sushi, that's that stuff that was once in the ocean, right? Never touch it myself but there is a good place near UO that I will take you to.

What I get paid for is almost all about education issues. That's good, but it leaves a number of universes open. It is the question of how to spend time that is most vexing.

Alan

July 28, 2007
Reginald to Alan

Dear Alan,

Congratulations on your blog, which I look forward to reading. I often post pieces or excerpts from pieces I have already published or are forthcoming, since there seems to be very little overlap between the online audience and the print audience, to the detriment of both (especially of the online audience, who at least in poetry seem to read nothing but each other—I actually read one person write that he only read poetry online, which I thought a damning admission).

Take good care.

all best, Reginald

---

[39] This refers most particularly to Adam Kirsch's review of Merrill's *Collected Poems* ("All That Glitters," *The New Republic*, May 7, 2001) but I have heard the notion elsewhere as well. Although Merrill had no qualms about his enjoyment of bouncing words off one another, poems such as "The Country of a Thousand Years of Peace," written to honor the 26-year life of his friend the Dutch poet Hans Lodeizen, are hardly superficial and stand comparison to the work of the best poets of any age.

July 28, 2007
Alan to Reginald

Only reads poetry online?! Good heavens. Well, that's better than not reading it at all. Today I rearranged the sidebars and listed some "recommended living poets" with links to your site and one other.

Alan

September 3, 2007
Alan to Reginald

Sorry I have been noncommunicative lately, I have managed to get all my deadlines piled up together, a bad idea. However, I also sold a couple of essays, which means a new tripod to replace the rusty old clunker.

In mid-Sep I'll formalize the arrangement and dates with UO, then later this fall I am going to donate all the swag to them for this appearance. That way I get a tax writeoff and you can work with one contact here (them) on the actual event. But I'll be in touch when your schedule is set so we can have dinner etc.

Alan
Nostalgic for Nixon....

Reginald Shepherd
"Working Class Hero"*

Because of the schools I have attended (all on assorted scholarships), because of my publishing success (it took me three years and three hundred submissions before I published a single poem), because I do not comport myself in a stereotypical lower-class manner, some people assume that I come from an economically comfortable background, that I have always known success, or that my success as a writer is due to social connections. Nothing could be farther from the truth. I am sure that everyone experiences a degree of cognitive dissonance between their own self-conceptions and the way they are seen by others. But if one is black, if one is gay, if one has been raised in poverty (as I was, in tenements and housing projects in the Bronx), if as an individual one has never fit into the various social contexts to which one has been expected or even to which one has hoped to belong, the burden of the distance between one's own sense of self and the fixed and often distorted images others have of one is especially heavy.

Though I have a publishing career, some highly contingent place in the literary world, that still feels as if it could be snatched away at any time, and my material life is quite precarious. I certainly don't have the financial security and stability I had hoped and expected to achieve by this age and this point in my career. I haven't done the things that one should do to be successful. I haven't networked, haven't schmoozed. I've been no one's sycophant, and though I would have liked to have had patronage, to have been someone's protégé (something I had naively hoped to get out of attending Iowa), that hasn't happened. I even foolishly removed the thanks to my teachers from my first book, afraid that readers would think that I owed my publications to them. Nor have I ever been a member of any club or clique.

Unlike the vast majority of those in academia or the literary world, I have nothing to fall back on. Since leaving my Aunt Mildred's house in Macon, Georgia, where I lived for two years after my mother's death, at seventeen, I have been on my own. It's vanishingly rare for someone from my background, having nothing (no family, no independent resources, no "home"), to have achieved anything in the literary world, which often seems

84

the preserve of those born with trust funds. English in particular seems to be largely populated by those who aspire to an Edith Wharton-esque, prissy, propriety-obsessed hyper-WASPiness: something which as I recall from *The House of Mirth* made all concerned quite miserable.

Several years ago I read a profile in *The New Yorker* of Jorie Graham, who as my teacher at Iowa once told me that I had had everything handed to me, to my ex-lover Chris Cutrone, a video-maker and critical theorist who grew up in a working class neighborhood on Long Island. He and I had bonded, among other grounds, as intellectuals and artists from poor backgrounds, people who as kids knew lots of words we couldn't pronounce correctly, because we'd only read them in books. Hearing about Graham's childhood in an Italian villa, the lavish parties her mother (a prominent sculptor once featured in a Gap ad) threw attended by Roman Catholic cardinals and Italian nobility, her marriage to the son of the owner of *The Washington Post*, Chris turned to me and said, "It reminds you that people like us weren't meant to be artists, doesn't it?" The art that saved me has so often belonged to the wealthy and privileged that it's hard to remember that it's not merely an ornament of power. Part of my project as a writer has necessarily (in order for me to be a writer at all) been to attempt to disentangle art's liberatory from its oppressive aspects, to remember that those who so often own art don't define it, that (as Adorno pointed out) art is the enemy of culture and culture is the enemy of art.

I had a dream that perfectly encapsulated my relationship to academia. I was in graduate school, walking with two professors, one an older white man and one a young hipster (swarthy, indeterminately ethnic, shoulder length hair, snazzy green blazer). The older professor was musing over some rhetorical question whose answer he didn't really care about (something faux-political, as I recall), but I tried to respond anyway, and the hip young professor put his hand over my mouth and said, "We don't need to hear from you about this."

As the John Lennon song my title alludes to points out, they hate you if you're clever, and they despise a fool. But I will be heard from. I'm determined not to leave the field to those born with spoons of various precious metals in their mouths (who nowadays include the children of the black bourgeoisie, however much they whine about "the rage of a privileged class"). The culture I've acquired with so much work may be their birthright, but I appreciate it in a way that those who take it for granted rarely do. It means something to me—it means everything to me. Sometimes I stand in the poetry section of Barnes and Noble and wonder how many authors there come from backgrounds like mine. They can be counted on the fingers of one hand.

My oldest friend's mother once asked me why, coming from what I came from, I thought that the world would or should be fair. I didn't have an answer then, but now I realize that it's because I believed that the world outside the prison house in which I was born and raised would be different. It was that hope, that faith, really, that kept me going, that keeps me going. Every "A" I got, every prize I won, was a punch in my ticket to that elsewhere. I wanted to escape the ghetto, but I also wanted to go somewhere better, which meant believing that there was somewhere better: my version of optimism, or simply blind faith. I have gone from place to place, from circumstance to circumstance, and still haven't found that fair, just place, but I continue to search, hoping and believing that there's a place for me.

I know that there are many smart and talented young people in the ghettos who haven't have the luck I had, the opportunities, or just a mother determined that they would be something more than a statistic, but I also know that sometimes the system that puts one in one's place and keeps one there with an iron-toed boot pressed down on one's throat can be circumvented, though hardly defeated. Indeed, if one doesn't come from privilege, one has no choice but to circumvent that system if one wants to breathe at all, and I have always insisted on drawing on my own breath. I am living proof of both the possibility and the precariousness of such an escape. I was not meant to survive this world. Many people have tried to crush me, sometimes with the best of intentions, as I know they have crushed others who have refused to know their place. I consider my survival a form of victory, however tenuous and conditional.

* For those who miss the irony in my title, seeing it as mere self-aggrandizement or self-pity, I point out the irony here. In the song to which this title refers, John Lennon means both that a

working class hero is something to be and that a working class hero is nothing to be.

Alan Contreras said...

You may not have any of those other stacks of toys, but you do have excellence, and there are those of us scattered here and there, including those like me whom you have never met (yet), who recognized that excellence for what it was from your very first book, who have purchased every book since, and for whom your name is on the very short list of standing orders at my local bookshop.

I read very few blogs—who has time, especially with a day job and my own blog and publications to work on? Yours is one, even when I don't have time to comment as I should.

We look forward to hearing you speak at the University of Oregon in 2008 ! I might even wear my upper-crust bow tie !

September 3, 2007
Reginald to Alan

Dear Alan,

I wanted to thank you for your wonderful comment on my post "Working Class Hero." I was quite touched by it. I had been nervous about posting that piece, because it's so personal and so open to potential misunderstanding as either self-aggrandizement or self-pity, but I was very heartened by the positive responses I received, and especially that some people said that they felt inspired by it.

Thanks also for your comment on the Stevens poem, which is one of my favorites. I urge you to take Stevens off your shelf and read around in him. He has some utterly amazing poems. Some people think his work [*gap in original, see below*], but though there are some frivolous poems (mostly in *Harmonium*), I find that the fires burn more intensely for being banked.

Take good care, and thanks again. I look forward to finally meeting this spring.

peace and poetry, Reginald

September 3, 2007
Reginald to Alan

Hey Alan,

No need to apologize for being uncommunicative; I have been very so myself, partly because I've been depressed (as the onset of the academic job hunting season always makes me), and partly because I've been sick (horrible kidney stone attacks and a scare in which my urologist thought that I had kidney cancer—luckily, he now feels "98 percent certain" that I don't). I've also had several deadlines, a couple of which I'm just ignoring. Bad bad me.

I didn't realize that you were putting up the money for my UO trip. That's amazing and incredibly generous. Wow. Thank you.

By the way, in my previous message, I meant to write that some people find Stevens' work cold. That sentence didn't make any sense as I originally typed it. Bad me again for not proofreading more carefully.

Also by the way, the rat seems to have been [a] one-time sojourner, and Robert finally nailed a board across the hole in the garage ceiling, so I feel much safer and more secure. Around here at this time of year, an unfinished attic is a pretty uninviting environment for any warm blooded creature anyway.

There were some very depressing stories in the most recent Audubon magazine about the sharp declines in many bird populations around the country. I couldn't get myself to read them.

Take good care. It'll be great to finally meet in the spring. I may have already said that, but it bears repeating.

peace and poetry, Reginald

October 12, 2007
Reginald to Alan

Dear Alan,

Thanks for your eloquent comments on my blog, and sorry
that I've been out of touch. I've been feeling rather depressed
and overwhelmed, have been sick on and off (terrible kidney
stone pains, which should be alleviated, since I recently had a
lithotripsy to break up the stones), and also have been traveling
(last month I had the worst and longest kidney stone attack of
my life while traveling, which was particularly not fun). But I
appreciate your good words, and thought I should drop you a
note to tell you so.

I hope that you are well. Take good care. I'm excited about
coming out to Oregon next year, not least because we'll finally
get to meet.

all best, Reginald

October 12, 2007
Alan to Reginald

Good to hear from you, and hope that you have gotten your
rocks off for good (that's a kidney stone joke, heh heh it will be
funny in a couple of months).

I have done almost no writing lately except for work,
though I had a call today from an outfit that wants me to do a
turista guide to birding the northwest for them this winter. They
are pretty well clamped down on my bait but they haven't talked
money yet.

I'll talk to UO again next month and get them working on
details. They are no doubt waiting for the money, too !

**[a message from Reginald to Alan about a partial colon
removal has apparently been lost]**

November 17, 2007
Alan to Reginald

Greetings, o ye undead po-master! Let the Word go forth from every rooftop that you, prince-regent of the period and Count de comma, are now a semicolon. But WHAT a semicolon!

Yes, I know, it will be funny in six months.

But in five months I hope to meet you. I just sent a note over to Creative Writing with my pledge of swag, and they will contact you to arrange something, probably in April.

I know you are probably tired these days, with hospital and carving, so I'll fade away. More later.

PS check out the piece on online dating on my blog.

Alan

Alan Contreras
The Ins and Outs of Online Dating

Some years ago, a friend with a dubious sense of humor mailed me a copy of *A Consumer's Guide to Male Hustlers* – to my office, in an ordinary envelope. The secretary displayed the calm professionalism for which we had hired her by opening and delivering this, as it were, disrobed object with my daily mail stack, offering no comment whatsoever. The book itself is a perfectly straightforward overview of the mechanics of hiring pleasure-boys and the nature of their profession.

Although I have never been in that particular market as provider or customer (setting aside the time when I, a college student, was offered five dollars to perform an unlikely act), I have wondered from time to time just what the less visible side of gay male dating was like. The advent of large, Internet-based databases for gay men to join and use as dating services makes the world of dating exceptionally broad, whether you are looking for Mr. Right or Mr. Right Now.

I recently joined a number of these services to see how they work and how they differ. I also attempted to arrange meetings with two men who provide what Craigslist matter-of-factly calls "erotic services"[40] in order to ask them how their profession works in the age of Internet-based dating. Historically, hookers and hustlers, mostly young, lurked on certain streets at certain times in order to find customers. Today it seems that at least the more upscale ones use the Internet to peddle themselves. Unfortunately one of the hustlers changed his travel plans and the other simply did not show up. I suspect that the latter was a student doing a research paper on people like me while I was doing one on people like him.

Joining the various services is easy. As a gay man, I only joined the ones that offered a chance to meet other gay men "in my area." It turns out that some of the services interpret "my area" to include the entire northwest rain belt: they gladly sent me profiles of "local" men from Seattle to Eureka. Of the services I joined, Dlist and JustGuys are free, Manhunt has a nominal fee, Gay.com a higher fee, Elitemate pretends to have no fee to start with but is all but impossible to use as a guest and

---

[40] Craigslist has discontinued this category.

has by far the worst signup process. Men4Rentnow, which might be called a special-purpose site, and which I didn't use other than to look at its setup, has no fee. The general-purpose Craigslist is also free. There are lots of other services, but these seem to be the largest or most active ones.

These services vary greatly in purpose, ease of use and tone. Most of them are straightforward dating sites, though Elitemate seems to be mainly a bait-and-switch site designed to generate names and addresses for spam and the like, as is Naughtyornice. Both of these use bogus posts to Craigslist as bait. My test of their various signup sequences made that pretty clear, though I gave them mostly bad info and they are now sending a lot of messages into space, not to me.

Gay.com is one of the older sites and has a lot of men on it, but it is brutally commercialized, poorly laid out, has clumsy, sometimes nonfunctional controls for moving from page to page and includes a cute little trick in the registration process through which it hopes you don't notice that it reinstated a fee that the registrant thought had been deleted through an opt-out. In short, lots of guys but a real hassle to use.

DList and JustGuys seem to be connected in some way, though I did not spend any time looking into that. Both are fairly easy to use basic services that have pictures, info about the guys and minimal advertising. However, they seem to add members rather slowly, which means that when I want to meet Mr. Right Now on Saturday night, the available faces are pretty much the same ones (in my "local area") that have been offering themselves for some weeks or months. These sites are heavily used by college-age men, perhaps because they are free.

Manhunt is the best all-around service. For a small fee, you get a very well-designed, user-friendly structure that is all but adless, has plenty of people on it who really are in my local area (heck, I even recognized two of them), and does not seem to generate a separate spamflow. The site seems to have been designed by people who might actually want to use it, and flows wonderfully.

Craigslist is, in many ways, the most practical, and is an increasing favorite among both gay and straight people wanting to generate dates in their area. It is also becoming a favorite way for prostitutes and gay male hustlers to promote their wares, as was discussed in an *Oregonian* feature article this fall.

One of the main problems I ran into with all of these services is that I don't speak the language very well. I'm a 51-year-old who does not own a television or a PDA and whose cell phone is rarely on and used with minimal competence. The combination of gay sex-term babble and text-message code shorthand (shortfinger?) used by twenty-somethings often produces a homotextual sputtering that reads the way my Scottish ex-boyfriend sounded when he got agitated: only half the words needed for meaning are present on a canvas of apostrophes, and they don't mean quite what they would in standard English. Reading what people say about themselves (and what they want in a date) can be as clear to an amateur as FAA tower-chat or the more arcane marine forecasts of the National Weather Service.

But in all this world of linguistic obscurity, fake photos, unlikely measurements, no-show hustlers and unrealistic expectations, I did emerge from this experiment with one actual date, a perfectly delightful evening with a tall, dark, handsome 23-year-old. So my commitment to research has had, if you will, a result with benefits.

November 19, 2007
Reginald to Alan

Greetings to ye as well. I am indeed quite undead, to the point (not to mention the period) of being quite alive. Actually, the semi-colon joke is funny now, though technically only a hemi-colon was removed. So I am, I think, at least three quarters still colonized. (A hemi is half, though, isn't it? I know less than that was taken out.)

Did you ever read the Dilbert cartoon in which Asok the intern convinces the pointy-haired boss that he should make everyone use semi-colons rather than colons to save space on the computers?

I might also mention that the Cancer Diet is an excellent way to lose weight fast. In case you were curious.

I got a note from Karen Ford regarding my reading out there, for which I am again very grateful to you. She said that the only available date in April didn't work for you, so we will do something in May, probably the 15th. I have teaching engagements all June, so I want to make sure to leave breathing room. It's so important to have room to breathe, don't you think?

It is indeed fatiguing being gutted like a fish, and I'm rather weary now, so I will sign off and go lie down. I took a walk around our suburban cul-de-sac with my sweet Robert, who is a whole panoply of angels, and am quite proud of myself for the exertion.

Take good care, and thanks for your good wishes. I look forward to meeting this spring. And I will definitely check out your piece on online dating. I never did that, but I did lots of personal ads dating in the Eighties and the early Nineties, which was sad enough.

peace and poetry, Reginald

November 19, 2007
Alan to Reginald

I think the fact that you were colonized was the problem to start with! I had not seen that Dilbert, what a great one.

Glad Karen has been in touch. She is limited to Thursday nights, and she's not checking the symphony schedule, but the 15th doesn't have any big drawpieces so she's probably ok.

Never tried the cancer diet. I'll stick to being a fat person, thanks. Maybe worship St. Atkins for a while.

More later.

Alan

Alan Contreras
Music for the Ages

This evening when I decided to play some music from iTunes while working on my latest book, I was surprised to see that "Sean's Library" had appeared among my choices of places to get music.

Now who might Sean be, I thought, and why is his library or any other part of his person taking up residence in my computer without so much as a "good evening"? Is this the next step by Dick Cheney to invade my personal space in search of terrorists? Then I recalled that this had happened once before, and represents one of the stranger aspects of sharing a network with others who have iTunes: anyone's music is available to others on a play-only basis.

The only network I am on, as it happens, is my own wifi station, which is also used by my neighbors across the street, three college-age guys including a Sean.

My next realization was that I was about to know more about Sean than he thinks I know. And he about me, should he download my music library as well. Then it occurred to me that perhaps he was getting my collection of, er, exotic videos also. Well, he'd sure know me better after seeing those. Fortunately videos don't seem to transfer.

Then the decision. Do I, well, peek? Do I really pry into someone else's musical tastes unasked? Granted, we are both from Tillamook County, but that hardly seems enough of a connection. But one little peek can't hurt, can it?

Well, here are some things I have heard of. Linkin Park, I think they did "In the End," a great song that I know from the On The Rocks acappella version performed at the University of Oregon. Metallica, not my style but I know what it is. But what on earth are Alice in Chains, Dashboard Confessional, Dropkick Murphys, Hatebreed and, really, Lesbians on Ecstasy?

But wait, what is this? Beatles, not a huge shock. Creedence? And is this really---it IS Magic Carpet Ride ! And this can't really be In-A-Gadda-Da-Vida? Oh but it is. Cat Stevens. Charlie Daniels Band. A landscape of Led Zeppelin and Pink Floyd. A tasteful selection of Queen, well, well. Vans Halen and Morrison. And yes, a phalanx of Bob Dylan. Bach in a cameo.

My duty is clear. I need to make sure than Sean does not miss out on Al Stewart, Imogen Heap, Aqualung, Colin Brumby, Lindsay Mac, Phil Ochs, Guster, Nero, Indigo Girls, Steeleye Span, The Pogues, Stevie Nicks, Shaun Davey, Ture Rangstrom, Philip Glass and Jimmy Eat World. It takes a village to raise the musical awareness of the young.

And those Dropkick Murphys - not bad, not bad at all.

November 19, 2007
Reginald to Alan

Dear Alan,

Just a short note to say that I was both entertained and informed by your post about online dating. What a Byzantine world! I thought that the world of personal ads was complicated enough (and at least half of my scheduled dates resulted in no-shows). Years ago I used to look at Hunk Hunter, which at the time was free and on which many people posted nude or even in flagrante photos of themselves, many of which one even wanted to see. I never tried to contact anyone (which might not have been free); I just downloaded photos. (I have about nine gigabytes of porno photos on my computer, which my Robert is kind enough not to make me delete.)

And now I really am going to bed.

peace out to the homebodies and the homosexuals, Reginald

PS--I also once had someone else's music library mysteriously appear on my computer via iTunes. I was rather disappointed that I could only listen to the songs, as she had several things I really wanted that aren't available anymore. You can go into "Sharing" under "Preferences" under "Edit" and turn off sharing. That's what I did, because I didn't know where this woman's music had been and what kind of viruses it might have picked up along the way.

By the way, Alice in Chains were an early Nineties grunge rock group, perhaps even from Seattle. I never liked them. I love Linkin Park, though, and "In the End" is my favorite song by them. Dashboard Confessional an "emo" act (really just one guy,

Chris Carabbia or something like that, who's terribly cute) of the "Do me, I'm sensitive" school. I've seen a couple of their songs that I liked. As for those others, the lord only knows, and he doesn't talk to me.

I'm so happy that you like Aqualung, whom I adore. And it was nice to be reminded of Al Stewart; I always liked "Year of the Cat." Except for Imogen Heap, Steeleye Span, Stevie Nicks, Philip Glass, Phil Ochs (whom I've never actually heard), Indigo Girls, and Jimmy Eat World (whom also I've never actually heard), I've never even heard of the other acts you mentioned. Which I guess just goes to show that what they say about the balkanization of the popular music landscape is true. On the other hand, I realize that I have heard of most of the folks you mentioned. So what do they know?

November 19, 2007
Alan to Reginald

I had never heard any Aqualung until last month when I came across a gorgeous thing called "Strange and Beautiful."

Here's to hunks, long may they wave.

Alan

November 19, 2007
Alan to Reginald

By the way, what is "emo?" I see the term here and there.

"Be naughty, save Santa a trip."

Alan

November 19, 2007
Reginald to Alan

As you can see, I still haven't gone to bed as I should. If I ever find out what "emo" means, I will let you know. I did a reading at Columbia University week before last and asked some of the students there, but didn't get a clear answer. I think it's music by "sensitive" but definitely straight boys who play guitar and may or may not wear eyeliner. Fall Out Boy seems to have something to do with it.

I too came across Aqualung by accident, having seen "Pressure Suit" (from his second US album) on TV and then backtracked to his first US album (which is a compilation of two UK albums, which I might try to track down). I adore "Strange and Beautiful" and also "Falling Out of Love," as well as "Good Times Gonna Come" and "Another Little Hole."

That's a good point about my colonization being the problem to begin with. Damned imperialist cancer! And now I'm partially decolonized. Does that mean I'm a dominion or a commonwealth or something, like Puerto Rico?

This time I am going to bed. I swear.

November 19, 2007
Alan to Reginald

You are clearly a commonwealth. Good NIGHT now !

Alan

November 21, 2007
Alan to Reginald

Hey semicolon, when does *Orpheus*[41] come out? Can't remember if I mentioned that your Thursday eve event here will have a book table run by the UO bookstore. You don't need to lug any books. The norm is to have a signing after the reading.

---

[41] Reginald Shepherd, *Orpheus in the Bronx: Essays on Identity, Politics and the Freedom of Poetry*, 2008. Michigan.

I sent the swag to UO yesterday, so the deed is done and U B Cumin. Knowing you and your work is one of the high points of my life.
-- Cheers - Alan

November 21, 2007
Reginald to Alan

Hey dear Alan,

Thanks for your note, and thanks again for setting up this reading. I'm very excited about it--it's nice to have something besides chemotherapy to look forward to. You'll be happy to know that after several days of what they call short-gut syndrome (in which anything one eats immediately takes the express train back out), my semi-colon seems finally to have decided that food, at least in small quantities, isn't an affront. I basically didn't eat anything the whole week I was hospitalized, so I guess it's understandable that eating again would be an adjustment. But I refuse to relinquish the benefits of the Cancer Diet (copyright applied for, patent pending).

Orpheus in the Bronx is coming out in January, knock on wood. That's what they tell me, at least, sans the wood-knocking. It would be great if you all had copies at the reading, along with my poetry books. I have an anthology coming out in January too (knock on more wood). I'm happy to sign books, before or after the reading. It makes them harder to return. :-)

Thanks for your incredibly kind words, by the way. I'm very glad to have gotten to know you too, if only virtually. You're an incredibly smart, interesting, and nice person. The blog has been an amazing thing for me that way, giving me the chance to get to know people I otherwise would never have met.

So the Internet is good for something besides buying stuff (though it's very good for that). It's also good for dates, too, apparently. I haven't been on the market in almost eight years, but I still reserve the right to be jealous of your date with a cute boy half your age. Did you get to second base? I hear those young ones are pretty randy.

peace and poetry, Reginald

November 21, 2007
Alan to Reginald

We rolled around in bed for a couple of hours; it was very nice. Not quite my usual type, a midwestern farm boy/linebacker type, tall and just slightly full-figured, with goatee, huge hands. And so very sweet and kind, which goes a looooong way in this world of snooty twinks and attitude connoisseurs. He even liked to hold hands !

He told me at the time that he was seeing someone on a regular basis, so I should not be too disappointed at his disappearance, but I am.

I see that Amazon is taking orders for *Orpheus*, which means my local bookstore (yes, we still have a couple) can order it now. I'm going to get one extra and drop it on the head of Creative Writing so she can experience your glory in advance of your arrival.

Enjoy your chemicals.

Alan

November 29, 2007
Reginald to Alan

Hey Alan,

It's nice that you got roll around in the hay with a cute young boy, and even better that it wasn't real hay, which would have been quite itchy and perhaps full of bugs. Holding hands at midnight, 'neath the starry skies—it's nice work if you can get it, and you can get it if you try. It's good that he told you ahead of time that he was seeing someone. I've dated guys whose way of dumping me (sometimes after standing me up) was letting me know that they were in relationships. Thanks for letting me know, chum(p). I can understand your being a little disappointed, but at least he didn't set you up for disappointment, the way I so often was.

Thanks so much for sending me those CDs, which I'm looking forward to listening to. You're a very generous person, in case you didn't know it.

100

I'm very excited that *Orpheus in the Bronx* is inching its way into existence. While I was in the hospital I got the spring University of Michigan catalogue including the book, which cheered me while I was in pain and unable to eat anything. I tell you, that cancer diet does wonders...

The chemicals haven't started yet, and I am not looking forward to them. I've heard nothing reassuring about chemotherapy from anyone. I have an appointment with my oncologist tomorrow to find out the extent of the cancer on my liver and the kind and duration (and side effects!) of my chemotherapy. I also need to remind him that I'm HIV positive, as immunosuppression is a side effect of chemo, and really I don't need any more of that, thanks anyway.

Speaking of doctors and HIV, I have an appointment with my HIV doctor this morning and should get going to that. Take good care, my friend, and keep the aspidistra flying. Whatever the hell aspidistra is.

peace and poetry, Reginald

November 29, 2007
Alan to Reginald

Hey semicolon, great to hear from you. I thought maybe some new music would help cut the dust of the trail, as we westerners say. We usually say it over something more easily poured (pourn? I think pourn should be a word, although I concede the possibility of confusion), but music will do.

Chemicals, diseases, various giblets. We are basically bags of saltwater with some, what is that delightful term, sweetbreads floating around inside. And we can only do what is possible with the terms and conditions that we are given.

Now, recall your liver to its duty by flushing it with perp-b-gone or whatever one uses on a recalcitrant liver.

My bookstore says The Book will occur in late January. Chemo will be nasty but you will get a nice lift from the book and will have all that behind you, and a freshly cowed liver (could I venture so far as coddled liver? Hmm, maybe not), when you come to Oregon in May.

Keep writing. That's all any of us can do.
Alan

December 1, 2007
Reginald to Alan

Hey Alan,

As Madonna somewhat ungrammatically says, music makes the people come together—music makes the bourgeoisie and the rebel. And anything that makes the trail less dusty is a good thing in my book.

As I was just reading in Richard Lederer 's superficial but rather amusing *Crazy English*,[42] it's odd that sweetmeats contain no meat, while sweetbreads are neither sweet nor bread.

I saw my new oncologist yesterday. It was one of those situations in which the reality was actually worse than the anticipation. After telling me that cancer would inevitably kill me at some point, if I didn't die of a heart attack or get hit by a bus, he refused to say anything about the likely outcomes of my very heavy duty chemotherapy, or even to be specific about the potential side effects and how to treat them. I'll need to have a mediport installed (wow, I sound like a car), and will have three days in a row of in-office chemo every two weeks for six months (during which period my health insurance will run out, which should prove interesting).

My surgeon told me that the goal is to shrink the lesions on my liver so that they're small enough to be removed surgically, but the oncologist wouldn't even commit himself to that as a hoped-for outcome. Only time will tell, he kept saying, along with, Either it will work or it won't. I kept wondering, if we're just leaving things up to fate, why am I sitting here listening to you? But I'm just inquisitive that way.

Did I mention that I have none of the risk factors for colon cancer? (Just the opposite, in fact.) And that they don't even recommend colon cancer screening until age 50? Ugh.

I am definitely looking forward to the book of essays, and to my new anthology (did I tell you about that?), both of which should be out around the same time. And I'm definitely looking to my Oregon visit, even though my oncologist basically wants me never to travel because it might disrupt my chemo routine. But I'm not going to be a prisoner of my own body.

---

[42] Lederer, Richard. *Crazy English*, 1990. Pocket Books.

I actually started writing a strange poem/prose poem in section the other night at around two or three, on the little yellow post-it notes I keep by my bed. I've since transcribed it into my computer, but I'm not sure what to do with it yet. At that point, getting in and out of bed was still an effort, so this poem had better prove to be worth it.

Right now, I think that a little breakfast would be worth the effort of acquiring, so I will attempt to do so.

peace and pulchritude, Reginald

December 1, 2007
Alan to Reginald

Great to hear from you ! Maybe we'll have to wheel you in to the reading room on one of those tall carts full of drip tubes: The Mediportable Poet Will Now Speak.

Liver cancer is not good, but then life is always fatal. The only question is what we do with it. What you do is glorious, as the world knows. Well, a reasonable part of the world, anyway.

Maybe you should find out if you can get any really good stuff via your new mediport !

I just finished Christian Wiman 's *Ambition and Survival: Becoming a Poet.*[43] Well worth reading. Images of poetry as a diving bell, for example. Major poets living in the suburbs of their gift and thereby fading. He, too, has a weird illness at a young age. I will do something on it for my blog sometime soon.

Alan

---

[43] Christian Wiman, *Ambition and Survival: Becoming a Poet*, 2007. Copper Canyon.

December 5, 2007
Reginald to Alan

Hey Alan,

I like that title. Perhaps I'll use it for a poem. I was never much for using the HIV shtick in poems, but maybe I can use the cancer shtick. (I do have a cane, after all, from some years ago when I had a knee inflammation.). L.E. Sissman got a whole career out of that. Then he died. But I guess everyone does at some point or another.

I would like to emphasize, though, that I don't have liver cancer, which I'm told would be very bad. I have liver metastasis of my colon cancer, which means that I have colon cancer that has spread to the liver. Apparently that's a much better situation.

This a fun week for me. Today I go in for a chemotherapy class, tomorrow I have my mediport installed or whatever the word is (I will then be officially a part of the Borg Collective-- resistance is indeed futile), on Friday I see my oh-so-charming oncologist, and then on Monday I start my chemo. So much to look forward to...

Thanks again for your *tres* kind words, which are much appreciated. But wait. There's a reasonable part of the world? Why was I was not told of this?

Christian Wiman is an odd bird. He's kind of a terrible poet from what I've seen, and I've read some incredibly self-indulgent and self-involved prose of his in *Threepenny Review* and in *Poetry* (before he became editor). He wrote a very nasty and unfair review of my second book in *Poetry* many years ago, but published a poem of mine there last year. And his wife wrote a vicious and comprehensibly ignorant review of my Iowa *Anthology of New American Poetries* [44] in *Poetry*, of which she's an associate editor. No nepotism there. I wrote an eloquently scathing response that seems to have intimidated her, as well it should have.

But enough negativity. My desktop has been flaking out for some time (never buy a Dell—I have a long and involved horror story with them), so I got a copy of Vista cheap from [*source deleted*] (it was six dollars or so). Now I'm trying to decide if I'm

---

[44] Reginald Shepherd, ed. *Anthology of New American Poetries*, 2004. Iowa.

up to the hassle of reinstalling an operation system and having then to reinstall all my programs and files.

Meanwhile, I must call my surgeon's office about my mediport. And eat some breakfast. Take good care, my friend, and talk to you soon.

peace and poetry,

Reginald

December 5, 2007
Alan to Reginald

I'm glad you don't have REAL liver cancer, just an off-brand impostor. Good luck with your technical improvements.

More later, I have to go to the office (ugh). I will probably do a review of Wiman's book on my blog. And one of Alex Ross's absolutely magnificent musical history of the 20th century, *The Rest Is Noise*.[45]

Alan

---

[45] Alex Ross, *The Rest is Noise: Listening to the 20th Century*, 2007. Farrar, Straus, Giroux. The review appeared and appears on the following page.

Alan Contreras
Alex Ross's *The Rest is Noise*

Alex Ross's "The Rest is Noise" is subtitled "Listening to the Twentieth Century," and that is an apt if laughably understated description. This splendid book is a must-read for anyone interested in music, and also for anyone interested in the ways in which music affects and is affected by society.

I am not a music critic of any subspecies, but I do listen to a fair variety of what is broadly classified as classical music, as well as popular and folk music centered around my own formative era. I know what I like and what I don't like, and for the most part I am content to allow such determinations to translate as good music and bad music.

To his credit, Ross does not tell the reader that a particular composer would do the world a favor by jumping into traffic (as James Merrill wrote of his wish that Schoenberg's piano would collapse mid-concert so the audience could flee), but rather sets forth the conflicts and changes in music from the late 1800s through today.

There are acres upon acres of fascinating cultural linkages in this book. The effect of jazz and traditional Negro music on Dvorak and various French composers may seem arcane and brutally old, but this week I heard the Eugene Symphony in my home town perform a set of traditional spirituals with the splendid young baritone Nathan Myers. The guest conductor, David Alan Miller, mentioned some of this history in his introductory remarks, and then proceeded to conduct a set of eight songs re-set with orchestra by eight different living composers.

When I saw this dangerously modern item on the program, I expected something that I could barely put up with between Smetana's "Moldau" and Dvorak's Symphony No. 8. In fact Myers was superb and the modern orchestrations were interesting and often gorgeous. Miller's comments could have come directly from "The Rest is Noise" and perhaps they did. History matters. History is relevant. History is happening.

Also here are the excruciating political entanglements of Shostakovitch, the iconic swirl and unexpected political difficulties of Richard Strauss, the dark musical involvements of

Hitler and his enablers, all in perfect balance. I have never understood the "why" of Schoenberg, atonalism and the strange unpleasant sound-splatter they caused and still cause in music, but having read Ross's history of this, I have a better feel for it. Some of it still sounds awful, but the reasons why we hear some of it even today are more clear.

Reginald Shepherd persuaded me to listen to more Schoenberg and give it a chance, and I was pleasantly surprised by his opera Moses and Aaron. So perhaps there is hope for me. Or Schoenberg.

What Ross does better than many writers is create and maintain connective tissue. He recognizes the flow of key events and adds only those side details that really build the story. I am reminded of such books as John Keegan's "The Price of Admiralty," Roy Jenkins's books on Gladstone and Churchill, Michael Barone's "Our Country" or Robert Massie's "Dreadnought." The perfect blend of detail, consequence and insight is rare, and Alex Ross is a master.

Just one example is his description of the Prokofiev opera "Semyon Kotko" in which "a change in Soviet foreign policy forced a revision of the opera's libretto. The signing of the Hitler-Stalin pact in August 1939 meant that Germans could no longer be depicted as villains."

The tone, however, almost always stays fairly light, with doses of appropriate humor, such as the inclusion of a scene in which American soldiers, not recognizing a bust of Beethoven, cause Strauss to grumble that "if they ask one more time, I'm telling them it's Hitler's father."

The long autumn sunset of Stravinsky, the long vernal sunrise of Copland, the clattering surge of twelve-tone sound and the late twentieth century advent of so-called "minimalist" composers such as Philip Glass are all here.

Ross is writing expressly about classical music, but toward the end of the book he begins including references to song and popular music. I hope that this is a teaser for his next book; little would be more worth anticipating than Alex Ross on the last 100 years of American song.

By way of epilogue, I sent Alex Ross a thank-you note, together with a CD featuring the Symphony No. 1 of Australian composer Colin Brumby. Ross, no culture-snob, sent me back an e-mail saying he had never heard Brumby before, loved the symphony and did I have any more Brumby? I sent him Brumby's piano concerto and two clarinet works, with the composer's permission.

History is happening.

December 12, 2007
Reginald to Alan

Hey Alan.

Thanks for your note, and sorry that it's taken a bit to get back to you. I had to go the emergency room (again!) this weekend, where I waited for eight hours to be seen. I've developed an abdominal infection/inflammation that had me doubled over on the floor in agony (wait, I remember that from somewhere, or somewhen). They gave me some antibiotics and I feel much better now (knock on wood), but it's delayed the start of my chemo, which is both frustrating and a relief. But I do just want to get it over with, and to find out what I'll be dealing with. Come Monday I'll know, or start to know.

I absolutely adore Alex Ross's book. I've loved his columns in *The New Yorker* and on his web site (also called The Rest Is Noise) for years, and I was so excited when I found out about the book. It's about the best book on music I've ever read. I'll be looking forward to your review.

Take good care, mi amigo.

peace and poetry, Reginald

December 20, 2007
Alan to Reginald

Hey semicolon, tomorrow is solstice day and a neewwww year is coming with all manner of good things in it including your glorious book and your Occurrence in Oregon ! So lick your chemicals like a good boy.

Do you have any interest in piggybacking an appearance in Portland onto your Eugene trip? Since you are done here Friday afternoon, we could look into a Saturday afternoon in Portland

and a Sunday flight home if you have any desire. They'd have to pay your appearance fee but youd already be here so it would not cost them any air, just hotel.

Alan

December 20, 2007
Reginald to Alan

Hey Alan,

Thanks for your note. Actually, according to my Defenders of Wildlife calendar, winter solstice isn't until Saturday. But I don't really keep track of such things.

I'd be delighted to go to Portland too as part of my trip out west. I've heard lots of great things about the city and have always wanted to see it. And if they're going to pay me too--well, all I have to say is, woo hoo!

So far the chemo is not so bad, though it burns my throat when I drink anything cold and today I got hit with crazy fatigue. I still managed to do my weight-lifting and my crunches, though I wasn't up to riding the elliptical trainer and it was _pouring_ rain all day, so I couldn't take a walk. They say that exercise helps with the fatigue and with the side effects of chemo in general, so I want to keep it up. Plus, I don't want to lose the svelte figure that cancer has helped me acquire--I weigh less now than I have in about ten years. I highly recommend the cancer diet to anyone who wants to lose a lot of weight in a hurry.

That's really cool that Alex Ross wrote you back. Somehow I'm not surprised--I've always gotten the impression from his writing that he's a nice and down-to-earth guy. Plus, he's a homo, which is always a plus in my book, unless you're a Republican legislator, in which case you're a lying hypocrite who should be taken out and shot. I will take a look at your piece on Ross. I'm thinking of doing a "my favorite books of 2007" post on my blog, which will _not_ include poetry (don't want to piss anybody off), but will include books like Ross's and this great book on the history of globalization, *Bound Together.*[46]

Okay, I just read your piece on Ross, which is very good. But I have to say that I think that you, like so many listeners, are prejudiced about Schoenberg, reacting more to the idea of his music than to the work itself. Schoenberg and Stravinsky were the first "classical" composers I ever heard, and it was they who made me decide that I liked the stuff. I've heard some "strange unpleasant sound-splatter" in my time (Robert listens to some free jazz, late Coltrane and Miles Davis for example, that sounds just like chaos and cacophony to me), and I don't have a great taste for what one critic has called "snarling dissonance," but Schoenberg's music just isn't in that category. And both Berg and Webern can be transcendentally beautiful. (Berg's opera Wozzeck is gorgeous and heartbreaking.) Anyway, I would urge you to listen to Schoenberg with more open ears. In exchange for the CDs you sent me, I'd be happy to send you some of my favorite (and more "listener-friendly") Schoenberg.

Take good care, my friend, and have a great holiday.

peace and poetry, Reginald

December 20, 2007
Alan to Reginald

I'll take you up on the Schoenberg offer. I have heard some of his work but not much. One thing I liked more than I expected, an opera (?) that I heard a couple of years ago. It was not Puccini, but it was musically interesting. Sometimes a challenge is good - we do hear far more Mozart than is healthy.

I got to hear the Berg violin concerto live a few years back, and although I can't say it would ever be a favorite, I got more out of it than I expected. Sometimes it makes a big difference to hear something live: I have only a very mild taste for Gershwin, BUT when I heard American in Paris live for the first time, it felt

---

[46] Nayan Chanda, *Bound Together: How Traders, Preachers, Adventurers, and Warriors Shaped Globalization,* 2007. Yale.

like a totally different piece and, although I'm not sure I'd admit this to just anyone, I kind of liked it. Shhhhh.

Let me see if I can get you a piggyback in Portland. I assume UO hasn't made your air arrangements yet? We might want an open-jaw ticket. It is GREAT to hear from you, drug-dude. Stay in touch.

Alan

December 24, 2007
Reginald to Alan

Hey Alan,

I hope that you're having a good holiday. I will definitely send you some Schoenberg, and maybe some Berg. All vocal, as that's where my preferences in all music lie. If you saw a Schoenberg opera, I'd think it would have to be either *Erwartung* (which is for a single singer and lasts about half an hour) or *Moses und Aron*, of which I saw a concert performance with the Chicago Symphony Orchestra conducted by Pierre Boulez. Sweet. We actually heard the Berg violin concerto, which I think is beautiful (and just a touch schmaltzy) down here with the Pensacola Symphony Orchestra, which is surprisingly good.

I don't much care for Mozart—it's all too la-di-da for my taste. I like many of Puccini arias, but there's a lot of cheese there too. "E lucevan le stelle" is incredible, though. Now that I think about it, in general I'm not much interested in thstandard repertoire, and particularly not the standard operatic repertoire, which is pretty cornball to my ears. Just call me thoroughly modern Millie, at least when it comes to music.

Why would you be embarrassed to say that you liked *An American in Paris*? We also saw a semi-staged performance of *Porgy and Bess* down here, but the Bess was very disappointing. Overall, except for the Porgy, the cast wasn't that strong.

It would definitely be cool to be able to swing over to Portland while I'm out there. I haven't heard anything yet from UO about my travel arrangements, so I assume that there's still time. May certainly seems a long way off at the moment.

Take good care, my friend, and have a great holiday. peace
and poetry, Reginald

December 25, 2007
Alan to Reginald

Ah, yes, it was *Moses and Aron*. Looking forward to hearing
more. Do you like Ned Rorem's songs?[47] I just heard from
Karen Ford this week. They will contact you in January.

We are expecting snow tonight. Actually not very common
here on the valley floor and kind of a treat.

Have a great holiday !

Alan

December 28, 2007
Reginald to Alan

Hey Alan,

Thanks for your note and your holiday wishes. I hope that
you've been having a great holiday season.

Moses und Aron isn't at all difficult to listen to, but it's a bit
dull, especially when not fully staged. But then, how gripping can
an opera about the conflict between two different conceptions
of god be? I will send you some good stuff soon.

I love Ned Rorem's songs, though from I've read of and by
him (including a nasty anti-Semitic comment in one of his
diaries) he seems like a preening, vain, self-important ass.
Luckily, I don't need to like him to like his work.

I'll be looking forward to hearing from Karen Ford about
my trip.

I hope that you enjoyed your snow. It's impossible for me
to conceive of such a thing as a treat, but then, I'm allergic to
cold and snow.

Take good [care], and make a snowman or something for
me. peace, poetry, and open ears, Reginald

---

[47] See "Ned Rorem and the future of American song," p. 33.

December 28, 2007
Alan to Reginald

I think he IS preening, self-important and vain (unlike us). I confess that I love his writing; I have most of his books. His observations are sometimes quite good. I like his Sym No. 2 and a shorter work the name of which escapes me.[48]

Alan

2008

January 21, 2008
Alan to Reginald

I read Adam Kirsch's recent collection of reviews recently.[49] It is an odd animal. He has real gifts as a writer, yet his reviews, for the most part, have a sameness to them, partly of style and partly of substance. He seems to have figured out what an Adam Kirsch review ought to sound like, and he pours Poet in one end and turns the crank.

I found myself feeling slightly undernourished by the time I was done, although his basic dislike of incomprehensible modern poetry is certainly congenial. Of course, he doesn't think much of James Merrill, whose work I like very much, and he likes at least some of Simic, whose work I can't get through.

Looking forward to your book.

I hope all is well with you.

Alan

---

[48] The shorter work I was thinking of is *Mountain Song*, for flute and piano, performed by Fenwick Smith and Mihae Lee, Naxos.

[49] Adam Kirsch, *The Modern Element*, 2008. W. W. Norton.

January 21, 2008
Reginald to Alan

Hey Alan,

I've read enough of Kirsch's reviews that I don't think that I could bear a whole book of them. He tends to make sweeping and usually dismissive comments based on a sometimes shocking ignorance. He's definitely very into being "Adam Kirsch," which is not a very interesting thing to be. As for "incomprehensible modern poetry," I'm not sure what you mean (or what he means). I like a lot of poetry that might be considered such a thing. I even write a lot of poetry that might be considered such (some people think it is). Who do you mean?

I'm sort of surprised that Kirsch dislikes Merrill (who is sometimes interesting, though the being very rich grates on me, as do the highly disturbing social ideas in *The Changing Light at Sandover*[50]—not to mention the ridiculous Ouija board nonsense) and likes Simic (except that I find Simic rather dull, which would work for Kirsch).

I just got an email from the folks at the very small, new press that's publishing my new anthology, *Lyric Postmodernisms*,[51] that the book is back from the printer. They're sending me my author's copies, so soon I will be able to cradle two babies in my arms.

You said that you were leaving a comment on Robert's blog, but I've seen no sign of such. Chop chop!

I just had the first day of my third round of chemo and have this neat new side-effect: I can't touch cold things without my fingers tingling and burning. And now even coolish room temperature liquids burn my throat. Fun fun. I wonder what's next.

Take good care. Is it cold in Oregon?

be well, Reginald

---

[50] James Merrill, *The Changing Light at Sandover*, 1982. Atheneum.

[51] Reginald Shepherd, ed. *Lyric Postmodernisms: An Anthology of Contemporary Innovative Poetries*, 2007. Counterpath.

114

January 27, 2008
Alan to Reginald

I see that your baby [*Orpheus in the Bronx*] is born ! Well done. My copy should get here this week. I have been horribly overpressed with work and didn't want to give you a casual response to your last note. With luck, this week.

Alan

January 27, 2008
Alan to Reginald

I was looking back at your piece on Ann Lauterbach. I think there is a minor typo that might be worth fixing as it relates to locating the article:

Your blog says:

"Quotations from Reality," *Diacritics*, 26:3-4, Fall/Winter 1996. pp. 152, 153.

When I looked this up, it is called "Misquotations," not "Quotations."

I am trying to figure out if this paragraph is by Lauterbach or is a quotation from Stein. Can you enlighten me?

> "The aspiring young poet begins to write in such a way as to invite a certain critical attention, to 'fit' her work into one or another critical category. This is the main function of being identified with a group or school, to draw critical attention that individual poets, not affiliated with a movement or group, cannot easily attract. 'New York School' or 'Language Poetry' are given brand-name status, commodifying and homogenizing, so that critics (and poets) can make general identifications and totalizing critiques without having to actually contend with the specific differences among and between so-called members of the group. Those not so identified are left out, often understandably embittered or confused, as the idea of an individual iconoclastic poet gives way to collaborative and tribal identities. Thus the

marginalized world of poetry begins to imitate other identity formulations which increasingly govern contemporary academic, cultural, and political life. Frightened by exclusionary clubs, the poet ceases to identify herself with the essential margin from which a vital critique must come."

Hope all is well. Snowing like hell here and several inches on the ground. We don't see this very often, and Eugene owns no snowplows except for the airport, which means that I might get tomorrow off, hope hope.

Alan

January 27, 2008
Reginald to Alan

Hey Alan,

Thanks for your note. I'm pretty sure that the article is called "Quotations from Reality," as I downloaded it from one of those online databases and that's the title is has there (I just checked). I sure hope so, since that same citation is my new book.

Damn! I just checked online and it is "Misquotations from Reality." I don't know how I messed that up, especially since I did download the article. Curse you for being right. Why couldn't you have seen this when there was still time for me to fix it in the book? Now the book has a glaring error in it and people will point at me and laugh, just like Nelson Muntz does on The Simpsons. Assholes. Mean, mean people.

The paragraph you asked about is by Lauterbach, not Stein (hence the references to the New York School and Language Poetry). If that's not clear, I'll have to go in and fix it. Along with the citation. Curses and drat.

Now I'm sulking...

I'm sorry to hear that it's been snowing so badly out there (I'm allergic to snow), but it will be good if it gets you the day off. It's been unseasonably cold down here—this past Monday morning when Robert was driving me to chemo there was ice on one of the roads (from spilled water). And it's gone down into the twenties a couple of nights, which is just wrong, wrong, wrong. Not to mention being wrong.

I've just started reading this book called *The Dirt on Clean*,[52] which is a history of Western practices and ideas of cleanliness—a topic close to my heart. I used to think that the Roman baths sounded really cool, but then I started thinking about all those people soaking in the same water, and now it sounds disgusting, like swimming in a public pool. Hopefully the grown Roman men didn't all pee in the water the way kids do. But still....

Take care, my friend, and here's to getting Monday off.

peace and poetry,

Reginald

January 27, 2008
Alan to Reginald

Well, deep regrets from me for imperfecting your day. I think imperfecting should be a word. I just now noticed that citation; I'd never gone to the original before.

When I read your piece I assumed that the segment was Lauterbach because of the references. The only reason I was a little confused and felt the need for a recheck was that the very last segment in that series on your blog has a Stein citation, while the earlier ones don't have any citation at all. I think that part will be perfectly clear to anyone in the field.

So cheer up and don't get your colon in a twist !

PS no snow here in May, guaranteed !

Alan

---

[52] Katherine Ashenburg, *The Dirt on Clean*, 2007. North Point Press.

January 27, 2008
Reginald to Alan

Hey Alan,

Well, I will try to untwist my colon and my knickers. I like that word "imperfecting." It's just about perfect. You should start a campaign to add it to the dictionary. I'd sign on.

I'm particularly embarrassed because I (mis)quote "Misquotations from Reality" not once but twice in my book. (Well, I guess I mis-cite; the quotations are accurate. But I liked the word play.) I was at least able to fix the citation on the blog, and I slightly rewrote the Stein quotation so it's more clear what it is.

Being right is one of the great pleasures of my life, so I hate to be deprived of it. :-)

I will hold you to your promise of no snow come May.

We're making fake lasagna (using squash ravioli) for dinner, taking off from an idea on Rachael Ray's 30-Minutes Meals (we love cooking shows and Food Network in general). She's annoyingly hyper-active and hyper-cutesy, but she has a lot of good ideas for stuff one would actually make, and could do so practically, even though almost none of it can be made in thirty minutes. Liar, liar! If I had a kitchen staff, I could make meals in thirty minutes too.

How do you feel about Kate Bush? I have a shrine to her in my heart. Also on my CD shelves and on my computers.

Take good care. I'm still rooting for a snow day for you.

peace and poetry, Reginald

January 27, 2008
Alan to Reginald

I've never heard of Kate Bush. I don't even know if that's a human or a kind of cotoneaster.

As for food, you and I are NOT destined for love: My kitchen is described by my friends as the place I store the pizza boxes. I never, ever think about food or pay any attention to it. I go to exactly the same restaurants (usually on the same day of the week) and order the same thing I had last time. Shopping for food is one of the great horrors of my life, and cooking, well, let us draw a kindly veil over what should not be seen.

I have a wonderful friend, Rich Hoyer, who is the great love of my life. I always thought that we'd be a perfect couple because he hates to write and loves to cook and garden. But he's still waiting for his Mr. Perfect (he's 38) and then there is the problem that he is Always Right.

I'd say 50-50 on the snow day. We had some melt, but not a lot, and should get more overnight.

Alan

January 28, 2008
Reginald to Alan

Hi Alan,

You don't like to cook and you don't know who Kate Bush is? Are you sure you're not straight? There's no reason to be ashamed if you are. Well, maybe as I look around at the world, there is...

Robert and I both love to cook, and we're both very good at it. We also work well together, and we've definitely made each other better cooks. We have two (small) bookcases of cookbooks, and we're always trying out new recipes, and of course improvising things. We rarely just follow a recipe straight.

Kate Bush is an Anglo-Irish singer/songwriter/producer whose first album, The Kick Inside, came out in 1978. Her best known songs are "Wuthering Heights" (in the voice of Cathy from the book) and "Running Up That Hill." My favorite albums of hers are The Dreaming and The Hounds of Love. You MUST look her up IMMEDIATELY. As in, RIGHT NOW. Listen to some songs on iTunes or something. She is utterly amazing.

Given that you know about all kinds of obscure music, I am shocked that you don't know of her, 'cause she's not that obscure.

As for Being Always Right, it's fine as long as I'm the one doing it. But I'm sorry that the potential love of your life is still waiting. Perhaps when he turns forty...

Kate Bush has a great song called "I'm Still Waiting."

Hope that you're getting the opportunity to enjoy a snow day.

peace and poetry, Reginald

January 28, 2008
Alan to Reginald

I will check her out This Very Day !

Does your cookbook shelf include the cookbook that goes with the Patrick O'Brian novels?[53] If not, I'll rectify that lacuna.

I kind of like the phrase "rectify that lacuna." Sounds like something done at night with a .22 down by the swamp. Strange splashings in the darkness, then silence and a whiff of pipe tobacco.

Alan

January 30, 2008
Alan to Reginald

Can you send me a copy of the scan of your book cover? We will want it for promo stuff down the road.

I just ordered Hennessy's interview book.[54]

Alan

---

[53] This refers to the series of "Aubrey-Maturin" novels beginning with *Master and Commander*. A cookbook that attempts to replicate all of the unusual foods mentioned in the series has been published: Anne Chotzinoff Grossman and Lisa Grossman Thomas, *Lobscouse and Spotted Dog*, 1997. W. W. Norton.

[54] Christopher Hennessy, *Outside the Lines: talking with contemporary gay poets*, 2005. Michigan.

February 3, 2008
Alan to Reginald

Hey po dude, I have put a piece on my blog[55] that may or may not be a piece of shit. If you have time, I'd appreciate your look.

I'll have pieces in *Inside Higher Ed* next week and in the *Chronicle* the end of Feb. I am glorious (this month).

My local bookstore promises me your book on Tuesday....

Alan

---

[55] "Hivewriting," see following page.

Alan Contreras
Hivewriting[56]

Recent commentaries by the late Reginald Shepherd, Ann Lauterbach, Adam Kirsch and Christian Wiman all include a concern about the tendency of modern poets, at least American ones, to write from an excessively personal viewpoint and to form hives that buzz in a similar way, heads in and stingers out, serving mainly each other.

Shepherd, author of the literary commentaries *Orpheus in the Bronx* (Michigan, 2008) and the posthumous *A Martian Muse* (Michigan, 2010) was one of the nation's best poets and literary critics. He comments on his blog (http://reginaldshepherd.blogspot.com/) on a book and essays by Ann Lauterbach, whose enthusiasm for modern writing is tempered by a growing concern that poets are clumping into identity-castles to the detriment of poetry as a whole, and especially the poetic audience. These clusters tend to write as though they are only poets of a group, not poets as individuals. Thus we have womenpoets, gaypoets, longshorepoets and other double-jointed po-beesten. As Shepherd points out,

> "Such fixations on labels and side-taking seem more prevalent in the online poetry world (certainly in the world of poetry blogs) than in the print poetry world, where things are much more fluid and flexible, though such compulsive territorializing and fence-building is far from absent there either."

Lauterbach's book *The Night Sky: Writings on the Poetics of Experience* (Viking, 2005) discusses, among other things, the concern that literary movements such as "Language poetry" or other identifiable trends can end up driving the poets, rather than the poets driving the movement. If poets move along in a huddled cluster behind a predetermined literary shield and don't go outside its penumbra as they write, are the poets really writing from what they have to say, or are they forming a series of moated guilds for the purpose of mutual support and

---

[56] This essay has been slightly revised since Reginald saw it. The original version seems to have disappeared, a victim of reliance on electronic files.

122

protection? This kind of branding or commodification is part of what Shepherd discusses on his blog.

Lauterbach writes of this problem in one of her essays (from the journal *Diacritics*) with uncommon clarity and a calm dedication to what words really mean that has become rare in poetic circles of late:

> "The aspiring young poet begins to write in such a way as to invite a certain critical attention, to 'fit' her work into one or another critical category. This is the main function of being identified with a group or school, to draw critical attention that individual poets, not affiliated with a movement or group, cannot easily attract. 'New York School' or 'Language Poetry' are given brand-name status, commodifying and homogenizing, so that critics (and poets) can make general identifications and totalizing critiques without having to actually contend with the specific differences among and between so-called members of the group. Those not so identified are left out, often understandably embittered or confused, as the idea of an individual iconoclastic poet gives way to collaborative and tribal identities. Thus the marginalized world of poetry begins to imitate other identity formulations which increasingly govern contemporary academic, cultural, and political life. Frightened by exclusionary clubs, the poet ceases to identify herself with the essential margin from which a vital critique must come."

There is so much of importance packed into this lens-hard paragraph that I hardly know where to begin talking about it. First, there is the understandable desire of a poet (or any creative person) to attract attention to their work. This, in today's world of poetry, also necessarily means links to employability, publishability and whatever level of fame a poet can expect within the literary world (not much).

There is also the general problem of narrowness that grouping inevitably creates. I sometimes write poetry about the natural world, and many of my friends have come to think of me as a "nature poet." That's how I get billed at my infrequent readings. There are some very fine poets who can fairly be classified thus (Pattiann Rogers and Mary Oliver come to mind), but I don't think of myself that way. The looks from my reader-of-nature-poets friends may get a little wide-eyed when they turn a page in my next collection and find a long poem about a 1944 naval battle off the Philippines next to a haiku about a college reunion and a dark reminiscence of my jury service in a child molestation case. I'm afraid my market placement as a nature poet is slipping.

Adam Kirsch touches on the problem of excessive narrowness in his recent collection of reviews *The Modern Element* (Norton 2008):

> "Today, the poetics of authenticity is securely established. ... Yet it should be clear by now that this poetics has thoroughly failed. ... The sound of the critical madhouse is a thousand utterly authentic voices, all talking at once."

What does it matter if you speak with an authentic voice if no one is listening, or perhaps worse, if they hear what you say but either can't understand it or, having understood it, wonder that you bothered to write it. Poetry needs to be more than just unplanned bleating: we can all make noises, but if the only purpose of your sound is to make yourself feel good or call attention to yourself, please spare us the distraction.

Finally, there is the matter of the "essential margin" and the idea of the critique. Movement-clusters in the world of writing almost by definition cannot abide critique except to the extent that another member may suggest better ways to carry the group's water to its literary destination.

This brings us to the fundamental problem of the moats, what lies within them and why it lies there. Do these moats protect a convent or a harem? It doesn't matter. In both cases the virgins are all serving the same master. It is not the nature of the group's master that matters, it is the existence of a master. A "school" of poetry is a master. A poet worthy of the name can have no master.

Shepherd's blog and Lauterbach's book discuss whether literary movements can become in effect a commodity. A literary movement can become a commodity, or at least a brand, to the extent that what its members produce is purchased or bowed to by a definable group of people. In the case of poetry production, that group may well be each other, within or hovering on the fringes of that movement, head in and stinger out.

What a horrible idea, "poetry production." In today's literary climate being a *successful* poet means being *employed primarily because one is a poet*—that is, paid to be a college-based poet instead of having an ordinary life and writing from that experience. In this unfortunate context it's a natural term. There are rare exceptions but this is the normal, the common, definition of success.

Writing from a group identity rather than an individual identity generates a certain level of safety, protection, and an uncompromising commitment to adequacy. This is hivewriting: the hum is constant and the result a good nap. What it never does is produce excellence. However, in that it matches the American society in which it largely operates.

We live in an age that is threatened by excellence, resists it (especially in education) and thinks any kind of clear statement of position contrary to the direction the bull is running is socially damaging (to the speaker) and unprofessional.

Poets by the hundreds have started building their careers by humping along familiar lexical tracks trodden deep with dust by the bull-herds. It is sad to watch. They all want jobs as protected college-poets. They want their extra-large photo in *American Poetry Review*, which would be hilarious if it were not such a peculiarly American way of establishing virtue-by-celebrity. Imagine where we would be if we had spent our literary column inches gazing upon photos of, say, Auden, Spender and Bishop, recorded for history by Isherwood, that ultimate pre-digital recorder.

Many modern poets become part of artificial moated cloisters constructed so that poets can run around inside them squeaking to each other like rodents turning a wheel. To what end? Although I understand and respect James Merrill's statement that he'd rather have one perfect reader than write for the great mass of people,[57] surely poetry written as a group

---

[57] Merrill's comment is reminiscent of André Gide's that "I shall let my books patiently choose their readers; the small number of today will form the opinion of tomorrow." *The Journals of André Gide*, Justin O'Brien, trans., Vol. 2, p. 275, 1948.

member for the group is too incestuous to serve any but the crudest needs. The fact that the phrase "career in poetry" exists as a meaningful concept in academe is cause for humor tinged with revulsion. But that is how poetry works in the U.S. today, in groups and with the same kinds of networks and cliques as appear in other employment clusters.

Christian Wiman, the current editor of *Poetry* magazine, in his recent essay collection *Ambition and Survival* (Copper Canyon, 2007) offers a clear view of what has to change:

> I have long believed, though, that to be truly ambitious is to be alone. Wordsworth says that a poet must eventually forswear all aid and criticism of his work or his ability to discern what's real there, what is most and only himself, will become too debilitated to function. Aligning oneself with a group is not the same thing as seeking criticism, but there is a way in which such identification dulls this blade of solitude, makes it easier to believe in what you're doing, and thus easier to become complacent.

The net result of this self-congratulatory clustering is that far more people think that they are good poets than is actually the case. The fact that they do not have—and can never have—a readership outside their guild doesn't seem to affect their understanding of their fundamental status. They are chimeras flitting in the forest of their own imagining. They embody the distinction between immanent and imminent: there is no destination at which they can arrive.

An astonishing number in poetry's legions are parading about unclothed but for their self-woven corona graminea. In their pride of cult they have forgotten that the grass crown of the legions cannot be self-awarded. Even the consuls could not award it. It comes in its own time, from the people who have seen with their own eyes the supreme acts which earn the honor. When we see writers crowned in chaff, let us say so. Let us award our grass crowns solely to poets of all schools (or none) based on their work.

February 3, 2008
Reginald to Alan

Hey other po dude,

I thought your piece was just terrific, and not just because you quote me and one of my favorite poets. It's funny, though, that you quote Kirsch in the context of talking about poetry and audience, since he was claiming on a panel I shared with him and two other much more intelligent people that poets don't care about an audience and only write for "posterity." I wrote about that in a post called "Readers Wanted," a few weeks ago.

Speaking of poets and their clubs, I just got back from the AWP conference, which to me at least was about the best example of such a club—everyone I met and talked with was really nice and very welcoming. It was only the second time I've ever gone, and I found it an exhilarating and overwhelming experience, especially since I pretty much don't talk to anyone except Robert when I'm at home.

Take good care, and keep the aspidistra flying. I think I already said that in an earlier post, but it always bears repeating.

Reginald

January 20, 2008

Reginald Shepherd
Readers Wanted

Early last November, just before my hospitalization for colon cancer, I had the privilege of participating in a fascinating symposium co-sponsored by the Poetry Foundation and the Columbia University School of Journalism called "Make It News," on poetry and journalism. My panel, "Covering Poetry: Past, Present, and Future," discussed both whether the amount of public coverage of poetry (mostly in America) has changed (mainly since the nineteenth century) and the ways in which the kind of coverage poetry receives has changed (mostly due to the Internet).

The critic and poet Adam Kirsch, with whom I've disagreed in the past (see my post "Final Thoughts on Blogging," in which I take issue with his sweeping and uninformed dismissal of literary blogs), asserted that poets don't write to be read and don't desire to be "popular" (he made this statement particularly about Emily Dickinson and the Modernists as a group), that they write for "posterity," and that only "history" will sort out which poets matter. I had to disagree on all counts. When I asked him about the role of literary institutions in these decisions of "history," he had no reply. As I should have pointed out at the time, "history" isn't an agent; "posterity" isn't an actor. They are the products of people's individual and collective decisions. "History," both prospectively and retrospectively, is what we make it.

Furthermore, it's a myth that Emily Dickinson didn't care about readership or publication. She was intensely ambitious and wanted to be read; she published ten poems in her lifetime (admittedly out of nearly eighteen hundred), and sent her poems to literary critic Thomas Wentworth Higginson in the hope that he would take them up. She also distributed her poems among friends and family.

The modernists all wanted to be read and appreciated, and they strenuously engaged in the work of producing their audience, of teaching readers how and why to read their work, through

128

essays, manifestoes, and anthologies. They didn't disdain popularity per se; they disdained the poetry that was popular at the time. Ezra Pound, for one, definitely wanted his poetry to be popular, and though he often doubted it would be—"Will people accept them?/(i.e. these songs)"—it disappointed him that it wasn't. He wanted his work and the work he supported to supplant the "ladies' verse" that he so despised. Though in one poem he wrote, "I join these words for four people," in the next line he wrote, "Some others may overhear them," and one may be sure that he hoped they would.

Pound's work as an editor (for *Poetry, The Egoist, The Little Review, The Dial*, and finally of his own journal *The Exile*, a well as of the anthologies Des Imagistes and Profile), and as an essayist and propagandist played a crucial role in publishing, publicizing, and disseminating the work we now call "modernist." As Lawrence Rainey notes, "[Pound's] gifts as an impresario were...impressive. Much of the coherence of modernism as an institution derived from his canny capacity to bring together patrons, journals, and authors, creating and then exploiting institutional opportunities" (Modernism: An Anthology, 39).

As music historian Arnold Whittall has noted of some of Pound's contemporaries in another medium, "Even the concept of music as 'bourgeois entertainment' was not rejected out of hand by most avant-garde composers, whose belief in the rightness of their radicalism was based on the conviction that sooner or later the value of their music would be publicly, culturally accepted, and that such acceptance meant performance in conventional concert environments" (Musical Composition in the Twentieth Century, 21).

Pound also very much wanted his social, political, and economic views to be heard and taken seriously. Pound admired Mussolini's ideas (if they can be called that), but he also admired Mussolini because he believed that Mussolini took his ideas seriously. It was Pound's commitment to those ideas, to social credit and the like, and his desire to disseminate them more widely, that led him to broadcast over Radio Rome during World War II.

Just as every good boy deserves favor, every writer wants to be read: otherwise there'd be no reason to write. To say that one writes for posterity is just to say that one wants an audience in the future as well as in the here and now: one wants a permanent readership.

I have no wish to change the way that I write in order to appeal to a wider audience, that mythical "common reader," nor do I think that such attempts to guess what other people want are usually successful. But I very much want my work to reach every reader who might be interested in what I do write, however few or many such readers there might be.

February 3, 2008
Alan to Reginald

I'm glad you had a good meeting and that you think my piece is unshit. Kirsch didn't exactly say that poets need an audience, but he clearly is concerned that a lot of what is being written doesn't have enough escape velocity to get much past the poet's own teeth.

I just had a nice roll with a pleasant 46-year-old. This coming week I think I have a date with a 19-year-old blond musclehunk, aaaahhhh. If he shows up.

In DC for meetings the 10-12.

Alan

February 4, 2008
Alan to Reginald

I checked out Kate Bush. Interesting and original. Not likely to be a favorite of mine because my taste in female solo vocalists is somewhat limited. Thanks for suggesting that I check her out.

PS I cooked this evening. Just so you know.

Alan

February 7, 2008
Alan to Reginald

Your baby got here today. I ordered two and sent one over
to Karen Ford so that she can be fully appreciative of your
gloriousness.

Alan

February 7, 2008
Reginald to Alan

Hey Alan,

I'm glad that my baby was delivered safe and sound. I hope
that you like it.

Did you know that I actually had twins? I have a new poetry
anthology, *Lyric Postmodernisms*, also just out. Amazon.com says
it's out of stock, but that's because they haven't gotten it yet.

I wrote a post on the Poetry Foundation's Harriet blog
(www.poetryfoundation.org/harriet) criticizing Charles
Bernstein, among other things, and got _tons_ of crazy people
responding (including Chuck himself, twice). That I expected,
though I never can anticipate just how insane people are, and
how _many_ insane people there are, because I'm not myself
crazy. But today I posted what I thought was a perfectly
innocuous piece describing and defining "post-avant" poetry, a
term which people bandy about all the time without saying what
it is, and got a _torrent_ of _insane_, _vicious_ responses. What
is up with these people? I've gone to AWP twice and met
hundreds of people who were ALL nice, and yet almost
everyone on these online forums is a nasty nut-job. Weird...

Why do you not like female vocalists? As a good card-
carrying homo, female voices are by far my favorites, especially
in classical music (and I always need the hook of a human voice
in any kind of music to which I listen).

Did you know Roland Greene, who used to teach
Renaissance poetry at UO? He was my teacher at Harvard, one
of the few nice people there, and one of the few who actually

liked and cared about poetry. I guess he's at Stanford now. I was thinking about writing him.

Take good care, my friend, and have a great weekend.

peace and poetry, Reginald

February 7, 2007
Alan to Reginald

I didn't know Greene. I used to be better connected to the UO, but many of the faculty I knew there have retired now.

I need to get serious about getting you a Portland gig. Portland is a natural place for you but the writing community there is somewhat hermetic and upper-crusty and I need to find the right crowbar to get it open. I do know Ursula Le Guin, and she knows everyone, so that be the best approach. If I had the time this spring I'd "produce" you myself in Portland, but I have too heavy a schedule.

I have to go to Washington DC Sunday for three days. After that I'll see who I can nag.

They'll put you in a nice B&B when you are here in May, but I'll drag you to my house for at least a brief visit so you can see your books on my shelf.

Female vocalists - there are some I like, Joan Baez, Connie Dover, Jessye Norman. I have always been a bad homo, though, in that I don't really care for a lot of them. Perhaps too much sameness in their songs, or the subject matter?

Alan

February 11 or 12, 2008
Alan to Reginald

I posted a comment to your latest blognote.

We have a solid offer for a reading in Portland on Sunday, May 18 at Powell's Books. This is the largest, most famous bookstore in the northwest and gets a huge gay clientele. Thus a good venue. They can't pay, but I can take care of your lodging there and any intercity travel. If this sounds good, you'll probably want an open-jaw air ticket (unless it is already reserved) into Eugene on Wednesday 14 and out of Portland either Sunday night (probably a bitch to get to Pensacola) or Monday morning 19th.

Are you up for it?

Alan

Reginald Shepherd
Gay Male Poetry Post Identity Politics, Part Two

As I wrote in my earlier post, I will be posting the presentations that my panelists gave at the recent AWP conferenc. The presentations and the discussion after the panel made me question some of my positions about identity politics and poetry, so besides the general opportunity to hear some very smart and talented gay male poets discuss their reviews on the issue, it really stimulated and challenged my own thought, which I found invigorating.

Obeying the law of the alphabet, I will begin with Christopher Hennessy's untitled piece, which started off the conversation on a high note. Once again, I encourage people to check out his blog,]Outside the Lines[, which approaches the question of the relationship of identity and creativity from many directions, and never with a sense that the answers are already known.

And now, here are Christopher's remarks:

"Gay poet D.A. Powell has pointed out that queer poets are "doubly displaced," both gay and poet identifiers fixed outside the mainstream. It's a location poets like Powell fully inhabit and one I'd like to consider today. Powell said, "In the America of the 21st century, the poet is a displaced person. The queer poet, doubly displaced. (Thanks America, for nothing.) If there can be a useful consequence of living as a second-class citizen within this growing empire, it is that the range of possible subjects and forms expands also."

Let's think about what the word "dis-placed" means:

1. To move or shift from the usual place or position, especially to force to leave a homeland: millions of refugees who were displaced by the war.
2. To take the place of; supplant.
3. To discharge from an office or position.

Each of these definitions speaks to a loss of power of

some kind, but, on the contrary, for gay poets to be 'displaced' gives us a perspective and experiences that can, if we hone our craft, strengthen our work. But how 'displaced' are we?

When I started to think about what I would say today, I found I kept coming back to the idea of normal as a location, what it means to be 'normal…what it means to belong to the club, what it means to want to belong--and more importantly for gay artists, what it means to resist that, to proclaim difference rather than to mumble or even pretend normalcy. What do we create outside the borders of normal that we could not create, or would not create, if we were 'like everyone else'? The key to these questions lie in what aspects of our identity specifically keep us displaced, keep us from being normal. even at a time when homosexuality is losing its stigma. (A hint – it's the sex, of course. More on this later.) I think these questions are crucial to understanding where we go from here, as it were.

In order to have such a conversation, I've 'brought together' several of today['s] prominent and promising gay poets to join me in a sort of conversation."

David Trinidad: I guess it's always felt like the things I shouldn't or couldn't say are the things that I must say. For instance, putting one's sexual identity on the line felt like a risky thing to do in the 1970's; it also felt like a necessary thing to do. I think it's still risky, especially since gay poetry has become (since the late 80's) more coded, more conservative, as if it's trying to pass (I think of gay men getting married, raising babies) as straight. I always feel (whether it's true or not) that there's something unacceptable about my poems — they're too gay, too campy, too middle class. And that unacceptability is a big part of what makes my work (I hope) distinct.

CH: I think it's important David has noted the possibilities gay people now have, the relative safety we

135

enjoy. Are gay poets trying to pass as straight? I'm not sure. We may no longer face persecution, but what about assimilation? I worry that being safe means the risk-taking, the boundary pushing, the edge-exploring will fade. Looking back, I'm thankful for the crucible of growing up gay because I think it's really affected me, in positive ways, as a writer.

Frank Bidart: To grow up gay in America is to know early that one's existence is fundamentally antithetical to the fictions desperately asserted by institutions that imagine their authority proceeds from God or nature. To know early that one's existence is fundamentally antithetical, period. That's a good start for a writer.

Joan Larkin, co-editor of the anthology *Gay and Lesbian Poetry in Our Time*: We are not just-like-straights-except-for one-thing. We are different because--often from an early age--many of us experience and see the world differently. Not separately, but distinctly--both the inside story and the outside story. It's often the gay writer who's taking risks for the entire culture. We're really good at that. From early childhood, many of use are faced with situations...we are forced to deal with....One of the daring things we do is write poems. Finding some way to tell the truth is part of staying sane. that's why our poems are often risky. And disturbing.

CH: In the past, we've had to create new metaphors, coded our language, disguised our desire, turned to myth and history and art as subjects in our poems when we wanted to talk about our differences--all strategies that refreshed the tradition, I think. And it's about more than that--it's about putting us in a position to see the world differently.

Mark Doty: Queerness invites us, every minute of our lives, to question our assumptions about what a man or a woman is, a mother or a father, a citizen; what is desire and what are the institutions we build around it,

136

what does it mean to be desired, or the one doing the desiring? The position of questioning can keep an artist alive. I hope to never lose a liberating degree of distance from conventionality.

Alfred Corn: A contestatory stance: this is a good vantage point for an artist. We can see what the mainstream takes for granted, and we may call those axioms into question. Where there is no conflict or contestation, art is banal. Conflict comes to gay people ready-made, and we have to make use of it, in order not to be overwhelmed by it.

CH: I agree. Of course, it's not always easy, but I feel like if we have something unique to offer poetry, something that informs our individual voice, whether we want it to or not, we have a responsibility to the poems to utilize it, to understand it. (Understanding that 'it' is why I do my interviews!) But as society accepts us more and more, do we risk becoming 'normal'? I would argue not yet and perhaps never. Because let's be honest, a big part of what makes us different lies in sex, desire and our relationship to the body, since this is what most explicitly and most fundamentally makes us different. Sure, our love is no better or worse than heterosexual love, our sex and relationships no more or less messy, our right to love and lust no more valid. But because of a history of repression, oppression, and sublimation; because of seeing the body as a site of death and disease for decades after celebrating it as a place of transcendence; because physically we do things that are, shall we say, a creative use of our bodies, because of all of this, gay writers start in what turns out to be a frustrated place-- a burning desire to speak about our love and eroticism but not knowing how to do so, and not being sure it's even safe to do so.

Alfred Corn again: When I contemplate the nature of sex between men, I find a counterpart in the art that gay men produce--a special searing intensity, the DMZ

137

between pleasure and pain, synonyms for which might be "ravishment" or "rapture." Also, the ability to play both sides of the tandem, to understand both entering and being entered. Art has its analogues to these physical / psychological states.

CH: I think part of our work can be to analyze those 'analogues,' to understand how our desires get translated in our texts. I like what Alfred says but of course that is only one way our lives, unique and varied as they are and always have been, offer the work. How else might our experience affect our writing?

Carl Morse, co-editor of the *Gay and Lesbian Poetry in Our Time*, talking about the anthology's poems: Some of these experiences require recasting of the language-- since no one has ever talked about them before--and these poets have done a lot of that. Gay and lesbian poetry refreshes the language. So much of this writing gets away from "polarity vocabularies."

CH: I'd like to think that our perspective on sex and desire gives us permission to expand the boundaries of poetry, to push what the lyric, for example, can accomplish. In the Michael Lassell and Elena Georgiou anthology *The World in Us*, the editors argue that our most important contribution is "the liberation of the libido."

J.D. McClatchy: Over the centuries, the homosexual temperament has seemed especially suited to engaging the themes of bafflement, secret joys, private perspectives, forbidden paradises, hypocritical conventions, and ecstatic occasions."

CH: I think it's important to note that McClatchy says "suited to engaging the themes,' not just 'suited to themes.' So for me, that means our talents lie not only in what we write but how we 'engage those themes', that is, how we convey our experiences onto the page. Well-known British poet and author of seminal texts on the history of gay poetry Gregory Woods argues that modern gay poets "have reflected the peculiarity of their social status by adapting correspondingly peculiar linguistic strategies." For example, in his *A History of Gay Literature: The Male Tradition* he explores how gay poets employ paradox. "Once one finds oneself to be para doxa, freed from the 'logic' of linguistic common sense and the 'natural' urges of the syntax we have been taught, all kinds of poetic dialects struggle to unfurl the tongue."

Our own **Brian Teare**: Though we often speak of experimentation exclusively in terms of what a poem does with syntax, the line, or the page, there are as many conventions about subject matte--and how we feel about certain subjects--to be tested. For instance, writing a good lyric poem about enjoying anal sex: that too is a resistance, a test of what poetry can do.

CH: I always think of Ginsberg in this respect. I read a review of his books once in which the critic said: "No other writer of his generation defended homosexual desire as a fit subject for poetry as effectively as Ginsberg" and doing so within "a vision of the world in which the asshole could be, rather than a source of shame, something deeply holy." I think that's an important function for a poet--turning a subject inside-out, upside down, from shameful to holy. But I wonder if today's poets are interested in that function, taking advantage of our ability to speak about those experiences that make us different?

Rick Barot: We're now in an amazing moment where artists can describe gay desire without having to camouflage it as something else. That desire can finally be an open subject matter, and this freedom has given us some recent writing that is scary, truthful, beautiful, and profoundly new.

CH: True as that may be, I think with it comes yet another problem, created, perhaps, in part, ironically,

139

because of the levels to which Ginsberg pushed poetry. It's that a deference to difference often times means that those gay writers who embrace sexuality in their work, depict those elements of our lives explicitly, are forced to worry if we'll be seen as abandoning the poem's needs over a "personal" (of god forbid political!) desire to 'make a statement'. Or maybe that's just me. Of course, that doesn't stop us from writing the poems we must!

Our own **Aaron Smith**: I've felt like being overt/explicit in subject matter in "mainstream" poetry has been an uphill battle. It seems like since the late '80s early '90s there has been such a backlash against confessional poetry that anything narrative, seemingly personal, and/or sexual gets lumped under writing that is just for shock value. The writing is defined by that quality and not assessed for its craft, skill, and overall project. And so many writers are afraid to write personally for fear of being labeled a confessional poet.

CH: I personally hope we continue to embrace our differences as well as our similarities, no matter how post-gay we become. On that note, I'll give the last words to J.D. McClatchy and Rafael Campo. McClatchy tells us why the difficulties of our history give us urgency and necessity to express our differences.

J.D. McClatchy again: [Speaking about the poets in his anthology of gay love poetry] Because their desires have been deemed dangerous, and their lives made difficult, they place a unique value on true love....Pleasure has been wrung from pain, illumination wrested from bitterness and fear, the moment of transcendence stolen from complacent hours.

CH: And Rafael Campo tells us how the triumph of our tradition gives us the permission and inspiration to write out our lives.

140

Rafael Campo: I realize that the gay literary aesthetic is one of hope, ultimately, where art is not simply a monument that displaces the truth of our existence, but rather is an insistence that we exist. At once edgily transgressive and universally humane, both painfully fractured and joyously restorative, queer writing is more than its artificial accomplishment in the eyes of critics; it is a document of persistence, an act of beauty, and the very breath and heartbeat of an imaginative and ultimately indomitable people.

February 8, 2008

Alan Contreras said...

Thanks, Reginald, for posting this interesting discussion. We look forward to your appearance at the University of Oregon in May.

I am a gay writer who writes poetry, though the great bulk of my writing is prose about higher education issues or ornithology. My poetry is very rarely about what I think of as "gay themes," yet I agree completely with the panelists who correctly perceive that gay writers by definition can't help but see society differently. I am IN society but I am not OF society.

I own every book of poems that J.D. McClatchy and you, Reginald, have published, and also all of Merrill, all of Carl Phillips and some works by Mark Doty. Many of the poems in these collections have a gay theme to them, but many do not.

I don't feel obligated to write about "gay things" because I am a gay person. It seems so cramped to limit oneself that way. Yet most of the panelists speak as though a gay poet has an obligation to focus on gay themes. Why?

Reginald Shepherd said...

Dear Alan,

Thanks for your comment, and I agree with your perspective. Christopher's presentation, the first I posted, is framed as a conversation, not a series of directives. I think of it as a conversation we are invited to join with our own voices and viewpoints.

I am no less a "gay" poet or a "black" poet when I am writing about house finches and pileated woodpeckers than when I am writing about late night cruising in Chicago (long in the past by now) or my childhood in the Bronx ghetto.

I do think that being or becoming gay has given me a different perspective, but that perspective informs everything I write and write about. Whatever I see, I see it a bit differently. But I see, and write about, a lot of things. I am utterly opposed to the idea that a gay writer should write in a certain way or on certain topics.

I've just posted another piece from the panel, by the wonderful poet (and one of my closest friends) Brad Richard, which goes very far in questioning (even exploding) the whole notion of "gay poetry." I think that you'll find it of interest.

peace and poetry, Reginald

February 12, 2008
Reginald to Alan

Hey Alan,

That would be fabulous if I could do a reading a Powell's, which I know quite well--there are a couple in Chicago I used to patronize all the time, and I've mail ordered from them several times since moving out of the city.

But if my UO reading is on May 15, that would be a *long* trip, really too long for me. Is there a way to push the UO reading closer to the Powell's reading? Let me know what's possible. I'd hate to miss this great opportunity, but I don't think I could handle that long a trip, especially in my current delicate condition.

peace and poetry, Reginald

[*followup message the same day*] Oh, I forgot to mention that I posted a comment in response to your comment. I don't remember exactly what I said, but it was good, and it addressed your concerns, with which I totally concur. "Give me land, give land, give me country that I love—don't fence me in."

Also, I'm very proud of you for actually making your own dinner. You might turn out to be a homosexual yet. We'll have to see how you pass the other tests...

Februrary 11 or 12, 2008
Alan to Reginald

I got on ABE this evening and ordered a copy of the Samuel Delany book you mentioned in your intro.[58] There were only 9 copies available in the US !

I am a big sci-fi fan and the only book-length fiction I have done (unpublished so far) has been that kind. That's what I'll do more of when I retire.

I have never read ANY Adorno. What should I start with?

Alan

February 12, 2008
Reginald to Alan

Hey Alan,

What Delany book did I mention in what intro? I've been writing a lot of stuff lately and I totally can't keep track of anything. They're all good—he's one of my favorite writers.

When I was a kid pretty much the only stuff I read was sci-fi, history, and natural history. I don't reach much of it now, but I love Delany, Joanna Russ, Gwyneth Jones, Elizabeth Hand, and Dan Simmons.

God I adore Adorno, but he ain't easy. He's easier than people think he is, though, if they just pay attention. I think that *Aesthetic Theory*[59] is his best book, though the only currently available translation, from the University of Minnesota Press, is

---

[58] Samuel R. Delany, *The Jewel-Hinged Jaw*, 1977. Dragon (hardcover), Berkley (paper).

[59] Theodor Adorno, *Aesthetic Theory*, 1984. Routledge and Kegan Paul.

designed to be as difficult to read as possible (no section breaks, and Greek words aren't even transliterated, for example). There's an earlier, out of print translation from Routledge that's much more readable. It can be found online. His two volume collection of essays, *Notes to Literature*,[60] is also good, and contains my favorite single piece of his, "Lyric Poetry and Society."

Take good care, my friend.

peace and poetry,

Reginald

February 13, 2008
Alan to Reginald

Check out my latest in Inside Higher Ed.[61]

Alan

---

[60] Theodor Adorno, *Notes to Literature*, 1991-92. Columbia.
[61] "The Risk of Reading," Appendix p. ___

Alan Contreras
The risk of reading

Our reading choices build our intellectual universe book by book, essay by essay, poem by poem. We who read are faced each day with choices about what, from the extraordinary delta of writing flowing past our life-islands, to pluck from the flow, set aside and (perhaps) read. How do we decide what is worth the risk of reading?

I use the word "risk" in its Vidalian sense: Gore Vidal has famously written that he only reads fiction by Nobel prize winners, thereby being assured that he will never read a bad book. This is the opportunity-cost approach to reading that brings the word "risk" to mind. We have only a limited number of hours in which to read. Some of that time is necessarily spent reading professional material which, although it may contain kernels or even nuggets necessary for our work, also contains enough mere dicta, the space-filling dreck and overstuffed furnishings of academe, that we don't generally read it for pleasure or enlightenment.

We are increasingly expected to make no errors in our reading decisions, to avoid side channels and to read the "right" books, especially because we are all short of time. Sometimes these books, the ones "everybody" is reading, prove to be exceptionally good, for example Khaled Hosseini's *The Kite Runner*. Sometimes they leave us wondering "what was that all about?" I have a list of the latter that my lawyer would rather I not publish.

It is true that my own tastes are suspect. After all, I have said many times that *Moby Dick* is a brilliant story up to the point that whales enter the picture. I know some English professors who agree with me, but they have to pretend that they think the book is great because everyone "knows" that it is. How can you get tenure if you think Moby Dick is a turkey instead of a whale?

There is a peculiar lack of judgment, or perhaps a lack of willingness to judge, in what we hear of books. It is pretty rare to hear someone say that a book is awful, especially if received wisdom says otherwise. But what is a good book, really? A good book is a book that inspires *you*, that resonates with *you*, that conveys a message to *you* that is effective. What it does for a reviewer at the *Times Review of Books*, Toni Morrison or President Obama makes no difference.

There is one way to resolve the question of what to read when presented with the stacks of new books that tumble like so much clinker-lava into our mailboxes, doorways and work-spaces. Ignore them. Take a break from the new and return to the books that have made a difference for you in the past. These are the books that have always spoken with a clear voice, have such a rich weave that different threads are visible in each new reading, or seem to adjust their effect successfully when read under different conditions or in different settings.

Most of us have these books to which we return, year after year, when the latest stack looks a lot like slag, the nuggets are oppressed by excessive overburden (I dedicate that phrase to the memory of W. H. Auden, who loved mines and geologic terminology) and we need a refresher in every sense of the word. Thus I return to Austin Tappan Wright 's *Islandia*, Patrick O'Brian's Aubrey-Maturin series, the essays of John Jay Chapman, Andrew Sullivan and (early) Gore Vidal, Asimov's *Foundation* series and the mysteries of Arthur Upfield (yes, one can profit from reading mysteries many times, if they glow with setting and humanity as Upfield's do).

The poetry of Carl Phillips (well-known), Cameron La Follette and Leonard Cirino[62] ('unknown') and W.S. Merwin (ultra-famous) meets my needs at a similar level: it doesn't matter which ones are the "best" or best-known. The nation's most gifted poets are not necessarily like each other: I might enjoy the rushing surges of Reginald Shepherd one day and the delicate brush-notes of Ce Rosenow the next.

I also think Frances Hodgson Burnett's 1915 children's story *The Lost Prince* ought to be considered a classic owing in part to a character called "The Rat," and I have read Arthur Ransome 's *Swallows and Amazons* adventures many times.

Likewise, there are some very well-known and successful writers, e.g. Charles Simic and Ray Bradbury, most of whose work simply doesn't reach me. So make your own decisions about my tastes.

It is true that we need to emerge from our lexical wombs and try new things now and then, but if reading a book, no

---

[62] Leonard Cirino is now deceased, but his books can sometimes be found.

matter how Great or touted, results only in a yawn or a who-cares, we are not obligated to salute it.

I recently had occasion to evaluate a formal "Great Books" program for a college in another state, and the school proposing the program seemed to realize that in this whirling cloud of iPads, Facebook, cellular devices, Blackberries and other electronic shrubbery, they need to do something to make books interesting to students at all. To their credit, they realized that the canon, although mostly traditional, needed to have its windows opened to let some new air in.

What do we recommend to young readers? Too often it is what they "should" read rather what we ourselves actually like and find most enjoyable and enlightening, not just once, but over time. For that reason I don't usually give young people books from the heavier or more ancient end of the spectrum (except maybe the *Satyricon*). I give copies of the things that I have the most passion about and that have made the most difference to me. I can't sound genuinely enthusiastic about anything else.

When I have given a young person one of my own choices, I often find that yes, nineteen-year-olds can and do decouple from their electronic universe to read a good book. There is, of course, an element of self-selection and cherry-picking involved: I encounter few dullards because I choose to avoid them. Yet I was once a fraternity advisor and participated in a round of pass-the-bottle with young people who were largely in the middle and lower register of the academic production line, and some of them read books, too.

We who claim that writing is important too often assume that students' lack of interest in course-related reading or books means that they are not interested in words in general. That is less true than we sometimes think. If we take the time to offer young people unusual reading choices that reflect our own passion for reading, we'd see that although the text may not be on their iWhatever, it may still catch the sparks that all young people have, and kindle from those sparks fires different from our own, but light, real light, all the same.

February 13, 2008
Reginald to Alan

Hey Alan,

Thanks for the shout-out in your article; I really appreciate the mention. I was reading your comments, and it's interesting to see that the problem of people running off at the keyboard without bothering to read or think about what they're criticizing isn't limited to poetry blogs. It makes me feel a bit better, actually.

Speaking of this reading, am I supposed to buy a ticket myself and get reimbursed, or are you all buying the ticket? In either case, we need to figure out the schedule. Is there any way the Powell's reading could be on Friday? I'm really just not up to a super-long trip.

What's the story, morning glory?

By the way, as I wrote earlier, I posted a response to your comment on one of my gay boy poetry posts[63] that I hope should address your concerns. The whole thing was meant to be a conversation, not a sermon on the mount of how to be a good gay writer, because I am SO not into that. Brad Richard's piece, which is the next one I posted, questions the whole concept of being a "gay writer." Check it out.

peace and poetry (especially, lord, some peace), Reginald

February 13 or 14, 2008
Alan to Reginald

I have a very special book to send you, ha ha !

I am also purging my shelves of duplicate copies of some things, do you want any of:

Recitative, Selected Prose of James Merrill

The Estate of Poetry, Edwin Muir

The Struggle of the Modern, Stephen Spender (this, which I had never heard of, is way better than his poetry)

Alan

---

[63] "Gay Male Poetry Post Identity Politics Part 2," see p. ___.

February 14, 2008
Reginald to Alan

Hey handsome,

I love very special books. Does it have naked guys in it? I like naked guys too.

I would love to have copies of all the books that you mentioned. (I actually read *The Estate of Poetry*[64] in college. It's good stuff.) That's incredibly generous of you. There are two Stephen Spender poems I love: "I Think Continually of Those Who Are Truly Great" ('cause, you know, I do, and even aspire to join them) and "Polar Exploration." There's also a really gay poem in his first book that I really like; I don't remember the title (it was untititled, I think) and I don't think he ever reprinted it.

People are still picking on me online, like the self-righteous blowhard Joshua Clover, but I'm trying to say that it's okay, because part of becoming a public figure is that there's this effigy (or several) of you floating out there that has your name and maybe even your face, but has nothing to do with you at all. That's what I try to tell myself.

It's almost time to for bed. Happy Valentine's Day.

peace and poetry, Reginald

February 14 or 15, 2008
Alan to Reginald

Joshua Clover, hmm. I have one of his books. Quite impressed with himself but an interesting poet. One of the "modern" poets whose work I sometimes gaze upon.

I get picked on online all the time. The diploma mill owners all over the world call me The Fat Homo and trash my reputation. That is because I am GLORIOUS. And so are y'all.

Alan

---

[64] Edwin Muir, *The Estate of Poetry*, 1962. Graywolf (1993).

February 15, 2008
Reginald to Alan

Hey Alan,

I have known Joshua on and off for over fifteen years, and have been close with a number of his (former) friends. He is rude, egotistical, self-righteous, condescending, superior-acting, and just generally an ass. He's also rich and has a tenured job, which makes his pseudo-leftist posturing especially hard to take (what has he transgressed or negated lately, besides the bounds of civil debate and reasoned argument?).

On the other hand, I thought *Madonna Anno Domini* [65] was a terrific book, and I've liked a lot his other work. (I invited him to be in my Iowa *Anthology of New American Poetries*, but he refused because it was insufficiently "transgressive" and "subversive," whatever that's supposed to mean.) His most recent book, *The Totality for Kids*, seems too much a set of notes to theory we've already read, thank you very much, though there are some good poems there.

He strikes me as someone with real talent who has consciously chosen to squander it, not to mention to waste his genuine intelligence on some weird nihilistic version of leftism that completely excludes the real world and real people. But then, so much academic pseudo-leftism does—these people know nothing about reality, and then attack me, for example, as Clover has done on more than one occasion, for being reactionary. Really, if I [could] arrange for him to be hit by a Mack truck while riding around on his skateboard, I would.

I need to get used to the online bullies. I got over them in high school, I should get over them now. Pretty fucking rude and homophobic, these online assholes who attack you. Do people ever think about what they're writing, if not before they write it at least before they post it? It's as if none of the rules of normal human discourse apply online. Freaky and disturbing.

Glory, glory, glory. That's us. They're just jealous. (I really think they are. A lot of people resent anyone who's done anything with himself besides whine and complain--which I do.)

---

[65] Joshua Clover, *Madonna Anno Domini*, 1997. Louisiana State. I concur with Reginald that this book is well worth reading and is superior to *The Totality for Kids* (2006, California). It is not easy, but it rewards revisiting.

Time for breakfast. Take care, my friend, and thanks in advance for the books.

peace and poetry and to hell with the haters, Reginald

February 15, 2008
Alan to Reginald

I think your analysis of Clover is right on. I have read a couple of interview pieces with him over the years and he reminds me a lot of the kind of gasping "liberals" who constitute much of the population of south Eugene. Latté revolutionaries.

One of your very great strengths is that you can separate the bitch from the litter (jeez I like that phrase) and look at the poet's work as work, decoupled (sometimes needs a pry-bar and a gallon of WD-40) from their personality. That is something very uncommon, if you look around in our culture.

More later.

Alan

February 15, 2008
Alan to Reginald

You can't play for safety and make art. See Clinton, Hillary.

Alan

February 17, 2008
Reginald to Alan

Hey Alan,

Thanks for the kind words. I do try to read the work and the person separately. If we couldn't do that, there's a lot of work (Ezra Pound the actual fascist, for example) that we just couldn't read. Even Chuck Marx said that Balzac's reactionary views didn't impede the insights of his work.

I asked Clover to be in my first anthology, but it was insufficiently transgressive for him. I hated him then, too, but I thought his work belonged. And I listed him among the "post-avant" poets in my Poetry Foundation post, which has now been mentioned twice on the *Chronicle of Higher Education* web site. They seemed rather bemused by all the infighting, but they did note that I had pointed it out as an issue. I'm revising and expanding that piece for my own blog, where at least I will get to delete comments that tick me off.

I'm so loving that phrase separating the bitch from the litter. The litter is often pretty damned filthy indeed.

My new New Year's resolution: not to argue with idiots and assholes. It'll be hard, but I'm gonna try, if only for the sake of my own mental health.

Since you're not into female voices (some homo, you), I won't even mention Dusty Springfield. But she will always be a goddess of popular music. And she sang a song about how sex in the morning gets the day off right. Please note my clever pun.

peace and poetry, Reginald

February 17, 2008
Alan to Reginald

My pun detector indeed located your pun and you are hereby awarded one pun-credit. There must be a word for that.

I always found James Merrill's utter detachment from the norms of daily life somewhat disconcerting (he is said to have never voted or read a newspaper), but he remains one of my favorite poets.[66]

You do a good job of focusing on the work rather than the worker. It isn't always easy. There is an odd guy in Eugene who is known mainly for what I will delicately call his attitude toward women, punctuated by the weird yard sculptures he erected to, er, honor a woman who lives on his block. Years ago (1979) I

---

[66] Merrill was not the only detached poet of the era. Robert Duncan once wrote that he finally voted at age 49 because he "couldn't stand the idea of Nixon being in... I was a perfectly honest anarchist before that, never voted." See Lisa Jarnot, *Robert Duncan: The Ambassador from Venus, a Biography*, p. 282, California, 2012.

remember him as the dude who would lumber into the 7-11 where I was on night shift, buy a carton of cottage cheese, stand outside the store and eat it by dipping his hand into it. But he was also the finest woodcarver I have ever known; his whales were found all over town. Not sure if he does them any more.

Alan

February 17, 2008
Alan to Reginald

Orpheus is magnificent ! Your gloriousness has once again been set in gold.

One thing that particularly stuck with me is the idea that the self is created (I am certainly a work in progress). I have always wondered why people allow Them to decide who we are, instead of deciding that for ourselves. Easier?

The mainstream: broad, sluggish and muddy. No shit.

The Stevens discussion was really good and may yet move me to read more Stevens. I have his collected[67] but have read very little. No excuse, just the way things have been.

Alan

February 17, 2008
Reginald to Alan

Ah, Alan, you are a true angel. Just like the song says, you're as sweet as Tupelo honey, just like honey from the bees. I really am glad that you like that book. Honestly, I'm proud of it. I should be—I worked on it for at least four years, longer, I think.

I've always thought of myself as a work in progress. I certainly hope so, 'cause there's definitely room for improvement.

Anything that encourages people to read more Wallace Stevens is a good thing in my book. He's a necessary angel of the first degree.

---

[67] Wallace Stevens, *The Collected Poems*, 1954, Knopf; 1990, Vintage.

Time to sign off now. I'm trying to train myself not to be online after ten, and it's already ten fifteen.

peace out to the homebodies and the homosexuals (I happen to be both), Reginald

February 21, 2008
Reginald to Alan

Hey Alan,

I've been hearing from the folks at Oregon wanting to make travel arrangements, but I can't let them know what I want until I know what the Portland reading situation is. If you could get back to me about that soon, I would be most appreciative.

Speaking of which, I am most appreciative of your putting this whole thing together in the first place. You're good people..

peace out the homebodies and the homosexuals, Reginald

February 21, 2008
Alan to Reginald

Portland can't move off Sunday so I suggest we kill it and do it another time. Portland has a major lit event series and I'll see if I can make them an offer they can't refuse for next fall.

You'll need Wednesday and Saturday as flight days unless you want to fly out late Friday and take a redeye east. I checked the schedules and they be ugly: two small markets not made for each other.

I have had the flu all week, I am vaguely human today.

Alan

February 23, 2008
Alan to Reginald

My copy of Delany's *The Jewel-Hinged Jaw* got here today and I have started into it. What a journey this will be. I can definitely see what you like about him.

Alan

February 23, 2008
Reginald to Alan

Hey A:

The *Jewel-Hinged Jaw* was, like, my bible in high school. I learned so much about writing and reading from it. It's utterly out of print, and hard to find used. How did you come across it? He has a new book about writing, called, reasonably enough, *About Writing*,[68] which is just brilliant. If I were still teaching, I would assign it to all of my students.

Did I tell you that when I saw my oncologist last week, during my fourth round of chemo, he said that the cancer markers in my blood have gone down from eleven to three? I don't know exactly what that means, but he's ordered a CAT scan for after my next round of chemo, and if the liver tumors have shrunk enough, they may be able to operate to remove them. It's good news, but I don't want to get my hopes up.

I also got a bill for $1100 for one month of chemo (I *hope* it was for the whole month). Plus the hospital where I had my lithotripsy in September to break up my kidney stones now says that I owe them $700, after insurance, even though I never got a bill. The woman I spoke to was like, "Do you want to set up a payment plan?" and I was like "I'd rather see an actual bill first." Don't you like the verb "to be like"?

It's getting late and I need to start getting ready for bed--my little rituals take a while.

Good night, sweet prince.

---

[68] Samuel R. Delany, *About Writing*, 2005. Wesleyan.

February 23, 2008
Alan to Reginald

Very good news about your glorious colon. Staying alive is expensive. With luck you will win lots of awards in the year ahead.

I ordered *Jewel-hinged Jaw* off ABE based on the mention you made of it in the intro to Orpheus. There are VERY few copies available out there and they are not cheap. I'm going to fish around the larger used bookstores in Oregon as time permits and see if I can find another one.

I'll order the new one. *Jaw* is wonderful but a little dated on the actualities of the s-f world. The great bulk of my unpublished output is sci-fi novels, and that is how I plan to spend my energy after I retire from state service in three years. Cleaning up and trying to publish the ones that exist, finishing two that are languishing half-cooked, and pursuing new ideas.

Alan

February 24, 2008
Alan to Reginald

Reading Delany's detailed comment on Ursula Le Guin's *The Dispossessed*,[69] I was astonished to come across a quote from a speech of hers to a lit club here in Eugene. She's from Oregon, of course—in fact she and I are acquainted slightly from many years at the same book signing event in Portland—but it was a strange thing to come across. She's not a bad poet and is something of a birder, too.

Alan

---

[69] Ursula K. Le Guin, *The Dispossessed*, 1974. Harper.

February 26, 2008
Reginald to Alan

Hey Alan,

I just got the big box of books you sent me. THANK YOU
so much! It was way more than I was expecting. The Spender
book should be interesting; I think I read some other prose book
of his a long time ago. I read *The Estate of Poetry* in college and
thought it very good, but I don't remember anything specific
about it.

Have you ever read *Camp Concentration* by Thomas M.
Disch?[70] Delany writes about it at length in *The Jewel-Hinged Jaw*,
which is what made me read it. But I don't remember much
about it (I was in high school), though I remember liking it.

Delany's essay collection *Longer Views*,[71] which Wesleyan
University Press published, has a lot of stuff about sci-fi, which
is what he calls a "paraliterary" genre.

Thanks again for the books. I need to contact Karen Ford
today about travel arrangements to Eugene in May. I've been so
sick this past week I've not done much of anything. But I will get
on it.

Thanks again for the books. You're a very generous man.

peace and poetry, Reginald

March 3 (?), 2008
Alan to Reginald

Hey homotextual, take care of yourself. I had the flu-slime
and it knocked me onto my keister for a week. If that's what you
have, just plan for a week of tired butt-dragging and don't push
it.

I have Brenda Hillman 's *Death Tractates*,[72] do you know that
collection? I am woefully ignorant of Ashbery - no excuses, just
haven't read more than a couple of items. I have *Double Dream of*

---

[70] Thomas M. Disch, *Camp Concentration*, 1969. Doubleday.
[71] Samuel R. Delany, *Longer Views*, 1996. Wesleyan.
[72] Brenda Hillman, *Death Tractates*, 1992. Wesleyan.

Spring[73] and that's it. Is he worth more energy? My attempts at Jorie Graham have foundered so far. But that is also true of Joyce's *Ulysses*.

I gave Karen Ford at UO a copy of *Orpheus* in order that she might be more fully exposed to your glory, and she immediately talked about using something from it in a class she is teaching. I'm not sure what got her all excited.

Alan

March 3 (?) 2008
Alan to Reginald

Just read your latest. Much to ponder. My taste in poets runs to more traditional sounds, though I stick my toes into modern waters from time to time.

Note error in citations:

Ross, Andrew. *The Rest Is Noise: Listening to the Twentieth Century*. New York: Farrar Straus Giroux, 2007.

Should be Ross, Alex. You have it right in main text.

Alan

March 3, 2008
Reginald to Alan

Hey Alan,

Thanks for your note. I'm glad that you like the post, even if the poetry I'm writing about isn't to your taste. I like a wide range of things. I hate a wide range of things too. Often they overlap. Basically, I like good things and I hate things that suck (in the bad way).

Thanks for pointing out the mis-citation. Andrew Ross is a big time cultural theorist (though his first book was about T.S. Eliot) whom I used to read a lot. (He was interviewed in GQ a million years ago or so about the semiotics of fashion. I want

---

[73] John Ashbery, *The Double Dream of Spring*, 1970. Dutton.

that gig, but cultural studies is pretty much over, unless you're a
TV commentator on pop princesses. I could do that.) At least
this mistake I can fix, unlike the Lauterbach mis-citation in
Orpheus in the Bronx. And today I discovered a typo in the book,
despite my and Michigan's copy-editors having gone over it
diligently. Drat.

Take care, my friend. I feel like crap (a nasty cold/flu that
won't go away), and tomorrow I'm starting my fifth round of
chemo, so I have a fun week to look forward to. Yeesh.

I like interjections. Particularly silly ones.

peace out to the homebodies and the homosexuals,
Reginald

March 6, 2008
Reginald to Alan

Hey Sunshine,

I am sick as a dog, or sicker, thanks to my latest round of
chemo, but I wanted to thank you for the terribly nice things you
wrote about me to my publicist at Pitt (who is an incredibly nice
and together person). And thanks again for sponsoring me.

Thanks also, again, for the books. I was reading the crazed
sea-captain cookbook today; it's pretty cool, though you'll never
catch me eating rat, whatever euphemism you choose to use,
with or without onion sauce. I liked the blurb on the back of
Robert McDowell's book[74] that slagged off "ornate
pretentiousness," since I love ornate pretentiousness. :-) And
Mr. Merrill really didn't write much prose, did he? *Recitative*[75] is
almost all interviews. Well, I guess he did write a novel. I even
read it, years and years ago. I recall nothing about it, though, but
I think I liked it.

I must lie down for a long time. Good night, sweet prince.

peace and poetry, Reginald

---

[74] Robert McDowell, *Quiet Money*, 1987. Holt.
[75] James Merrill, *Recitative*, 1986. North Point. Reprinted in J. D. McClatchy
and Stephen Yenser, eds., *Collected Prose of James Merrill*, 2004. Knopf.

March 6, 2008
Alan to Reginald

Good to hear your voice, as it were.

Reading your latest blog, and also the latest Oregon poetry society newsletter, I find the same word: emerging. I find myself wondering just what constitutes an emerging poet. Some (you, Merrill, Phillips, Ashbery come to mind) were clearly the Full Meal Deal from the very beginning. There wasn't any real question of qualitative status. Others start out as what you might call journeyman poets and build a reputation slowly over time.

What constitutes emergence? Quality, quantity, recognition by some particular high court of words?

I may blog on this question at some point. Any thoughts?

PS, we don't say rat, we say "miller" to make them taste better.[76] And what better revenge than a good stir-fry (remove tail and feet) ? !!!!

See you soon. Alan

Probably early April, 2008
Alan to Reginald

Congrats on your Guggenheim, though I really don't know what it entails. Stacks of swag and some public notice, I hope.

See you soon.

"Every time I hear a political speech or I read those of our leaders, I am horrified at having, for years, heard nothing which sounded human. It is always the same words telling the same lies. And the fact that men accept this, that the people's anger has not destroyed these hollow clowns, strikes me as proof that men attribute no importance to the way they are governed; that they gamble—yes, gamble—

---

[76] My comment on "millers" is an unattributed reference (sounds nicer than "theft") to a piece of dialogue in one of Patrick O'Brian's Aubrey-Maturin novels. I had just sent Reginald the cookbook that included recipes for all of the foods included in the novels.

with a whole part of their life and their so-called 'vital interests'." [77]

Albert Camus, 1937

Alan

April 3, 2008
Reginald to Alan

Hey Alan,

The Guggenheim involves lots of prestige and a nice chunk of money—I don't know exactly how much, but they say that their fellowships "average" $39,000, which is several years' income for me. Most of that will go to my ever-mounting medical bills, especially now that my COBRA group coverage is running out and I'm switching to a much more expensive individual policy.

"Swag" is a funny word. Where does it come from? Is it because one swaggers when one's rich? I see Bill Gates doing that all the time. Bastard...

Take good care, and see you soon.

peace and poetry, Reginald

[Shepherd had a serious medical relapse shortly after and had to cancel his appearance in Oregon]

June 9, 2008
Alan to Reginald

Greetings. I trust that you remain undead.

I am taking a week off to avoid my duties and get some birding, reading and writing done. So far not very productive, but I just posted a little promo blurb for *Orpheus* on my blog,

---

[77] Albert Camus, *Notebooks 1935-1942*, p. 42. 1965, Modern Library.

which must be read by, oh, ten people monthly. Hope the book is doing well.

And are you doing well? Send me a note when you can.

Parini's *Why Poetry Matters* [78] is pretty good. I wasn't sure what to expect, since I don't always like his essays.

I have attached a photo of where I am, my retreat locale for 38 years now,[79] and a pic of me being productive.

Alan

---

[78] Jay Parini, *Why Poetry Matters*, 2008. Yale.
[79] Malheur Field Station, Oregon.

Alan Contreras
Reginald Shepherd's Orpheus

I am pleased to recommend the following:

Orpheus in the Bronx Essays on Identity, Politics and the Freedom of Poetry

Reginald Shepherd

This is Shepherd's first full-length collection of essays related to poetry and the creative arts, and it brings his usual brilliance and clarity to bear on a wide variety of issues:

"A poem has never oppressed anyone, though I was once on a panel at a gay writers' conference with a black lesbian performance poet who implied that literacy was oppressive to black people, which certainly would have been news to the slave-owners who tried to keep their property from learning to read."

This is the kind of blow-off-the-cultural-cobwebs-with-a-jet-turbine writing that is rare in most books and common in *Orpheus*. Shepherd, whose identity is made the old-fashioned way, with original work, has a great deal to say about identity poetry based on collective defense perimeters rather than true individuality. He also discusses the nature of the urban experience and its connection to poetry, why he has chosen to write and other topics of interest to anyone who writes or reads poetry.

The book also contains exceptionally perceptive commentary on the work of Alvin Feinman, Genet, Wallace Stevens, Linda Gregg, Samuel R. Delany, Aaron Shurin, Donald Britton, Tim Dlugos, D. A. Powell and Jorie Graham. Graham is a poet whose work I have always had trouble appreciating: thanks to Shepherd, I can approach her work from a new angle that may shed more light than the old ones.

Shepherd also provides a useful mirror to what really happens in today's writing, for example:

"...much mainstream American poetry (and there is indeed a mainstream, broad, sluggish and muddy) seems never to have heard of modernism (or even, in too many cases, of Keats), retailing equally aimless examples of therapeutic self-exploration or convenient epiphanies in prosaic anecdotes not interesting or shapely enough to be short stories: what has been called the 'I look out the window and I am important (or sensitive)' school."

Buy it. Read it.

June 10-11, 2008[80]
Reginald to Alan

Hey Alan,

I am indeed still among the not-dead, though very much among the walking wounded (also a wonderful song by Everything But the Girl), with fever, fatigue, nausea and vomiting, a deep cough, and general cruddiness. I'd been taken off the IV antibiotics, but now have been put back on them, because I clearly need them. They're definitely helping. And Robert is, as usual, a whole hierarchy of angels. He really takes care of me. I tell him that I won't want to be a burden to him (I can't do much for myself), and he says I'm not, but it's all definitely stressful for him as well.

Thanks for your kind words about *Orpheus in the Bronx* on your blog, which are much appreciated, and which were also pointed out to me by someone else. Just so you'll know that people do read your blog.

From the photo your retreat looks beautiful. I was slightly apprehensive about opening the picture of you being productive, because I thought it might be a picture of you masturbating, which would have been too much information. Ha ha, that is a joke. Just in case. It's so easy to misread tone in email.

I am going to sign off now and get ready for bed, which I should have already started—my night time rituals always take longer than I think they will. Everything I do takes longer than I think it will.

Take good care, my friend, and I hope to finally meet you next year.

peace and poetry, Reginald

I just remembered that the "someone" who pointed me toward your blog entry on *Orpheus* was Samuel R. Delany. Now you're playing with the big boys.

---

[80] The June 10-11 messages were originally received out of order but have been arranged here in proper sequence, with a couple of inquiries about the sequence deleted.

June 10-11, 2008
Alan to Reginald

Oh my. Delany. What does one say? I suddenly remember what a very sloppy writer I often am.

It is so very good to hear your voice. More later.

Alan

June 10-11, 2008
Alan to Reginald

My retreat is unique. Ancient house trailers planted in the desert fifty years ago, adjacent to dorms set up as a CCC camp by the Roosevelt administration.[81] The field station is located at Malheur National Wildlife Refuge, which means that I spend the mornings having fabulous birding and the afternoons being productive - in theory. There is also a generous supply of mosquitos from late May through early September.

This site is rather isolated - 298 miles from my home - the nearest supermarket is 35 miles away (gas and convenience store 6 miles) and the nearest airports are Boise 160 miles to the east, Redmond 160 miles northwest or Winnemucca, Nevada 200 miles south.

I love coming here in the fall. So very quiet, no mosquitos, generally clear skies at 4000 feet elevation with the milky way overwhelming above. I hope to come back for 2-4 weeks this fall if all goes well.

No, I would not send you a jerk-off photo ! Not my style.

Rest. We'll chat soon.

Alan

---

[81] My error. The Malheur Field Station dorm complex dates from the 1960s and was a Job Corps site. Winnemucca, as it turns out, has no commercial air service anyway.

Late June, 2008
Alan to Reginald

The Olympic trials are underway here, and the hot weather has brought out SKIN in profusion, yahoooooo ! I hope that you are doing well.

Adam Kirsch's new collection *Invasions*[82] has some good poems in it. I like his poetry better than his criticism.

I sent you a few books maybe a month or six weeks back. Did they get there? I know you probably have a pile of stuff.

Looks like I'll be able to escape the office for FOUR WEEKS this fall, sneaking off to the desert and spending mornings birding, afternoons doing work for my office via the field station's wifi tower and evenings working on my own writing. Ahhhhh....

If it were not for the patterns in life, improvisations would not be noticed.

Alan

June 27, 2008
Reginald to Alan

Hi Alan,

Well, I'm sure it's nice for you to be surrounded by nice human scenery. I was just telling my friend Merav this afternoon that I really want to live somewhere with a) smart people, b) attractive people, and c) gay boys. Pensacola doesn't really cut it on any of those counts.

I did indeed get the package you sent me, including the copy of your book, but it was during my more-than-a-month-long sojourn in the hospital (I'm sure you know about that--if not, I'll be happy to share my near-death experience with you).

I am slowly and fairly steadily recovering, though with frequent setbacks. The nausea and fatigue caused by the daily IV antibiotic infusions which are supposed to help me get better are not fun.

---

[82] Adam Kirsch, *Invasions*, 2008. Ivan R. Dee, Chicago.

I've decided that I'm getting bored with "avant-garde"/"experimental" poetry. I like poems that have something to say, that are about something. But they have to be beautiful, which rules out most such poems. Or most poems period. But lately I can't concentrate to read poetry at all, so at the moment it's a moot point.

I got a royalty check from Michigan for *Orpheus in the Bronx*. You like me, you really like me!

It's getting late and I need to go to bed (see above re: fatigue). Take good care, my friend, and enjoy your four weeks of vacation.

peace and poetry, Reginald

June 28 2008
Alan to Reginald

No, Pensacola is not the pulsing heart of culture or skin. The job market being weird and your partner having a Real Job must be somewhat constricting.

Congrats on the royalty payment. There is something very comforting about the phrase "check enclosed." Mine is due from Oregon State U Press in a few weeks. It will be maybe $75 or so, since my bird books have all been out for a while, but hey, that's a nice offset to gas prices.

More later.

Alan

August 7, 2008
Alan to Reginald

Hey favorite fruit, good to see you posting. How is your much-perforated person these days?

Have you reconnected with UO regarding a visit this year? The airfare is good through early May 09. I'll be out of town Sep 13-Oct 10 and hope to see you sometime after that.

Alan

August 8, 2008
Reginald to Alan

Hey Alan,

Thanks for your note and good wishes. I just got out of a three-week stint in the hospital for surgery to fix an abdominal fistula (I was leaking fecal matter from my colon to a hole in my abdomen—fun fun). Since then I've been going to my doctor's office every morning for two and a half hours to do medication infusions, but now they say I can do the infusions at home (as I'm sure I always could have), which will make my life *much* better.

What with this whole new set of required recovery, something in the spring sounds like it would make the most sense, if you let Karen Ford. I really am determined to get out there one of these years...

Take care, mein freund, and enjoy your vacation, if that is indeed what it is.

peace and poetry,

Reginald

September 1, 2008
Alan to Reginald

Hey R. I hope the hurricane goes where you are not.

Just saw this [Willamette University] job announcement. Perhaps you or someone you know would be interested. They might take an MFA with a good record.

1. African American Literature
2. Ethnic American Literature
3. Poetry & Creative Writing

Three positions are available, one in each area of interest listed. Publications in the field are required & for Poetry & Creative writing a PhD in literature, emphasizing poetry, preferably from the 19th century to present is required.

Review begins Nov. 7, 2008 for all positions. Interviews will be conducted at the MLA in San Francisco between Dec. 27 and Dec. 30, 2008.

Alan

Conclusion

Reginald Shepherd died on September 10, 2008. I did not realize at the time of my September 1 message that he was in the final stages of his disease. We never met. I feel the absence of that meeting as a great weight. For some reason I kept almost every e-mail we sent back and forth, as though I had a premonition. I have never done this with another correspondent. Seldom have I encountered such a pure, shining intelligence. Seldom, too, a person less ready to depart, which makes his loss seem unjust.

Reginald once sent me an e-mail addressed to "Sunshine" and concluded with "Goodnight, sweet prince," but even that one ended with his unique good-bye, so with his words I must say my good-bye: "peace and poetry" forever, my unmet friend.

Alan Contreras

Fernando Pessoa

Antinous

Fernando Pessoa (1888-1935) wrote "Antinous" in English in 1918, but the story of Emperor Hadrian and his young male friend Antinous dates from 130 AD, when it both began and ended. In that year Emperor Hadrian, 54, lost his beloved companion at the age of 18, presumably to drowning in the Nile. Royston Lambert's extraordinary biographical history of the relationship of Hadrian and Antinous, *Beloved and God* (1984), their times and how Antinous has been represented to us over the centuries is the best source for more information. Also see Marguerite Yourcenar's remarkable creation, *Memoirs of Hadrian*.

Antinous

The rain outside was cold in Hadrian's soul.

The boy lay dead
On the low couch, on whose denuded whole,
To Hadrian's eyes, whose sorrow was a dread,
The shadowy light of Death's eclipse was shed.
The boy lay dead, and the day seemed a night
Outside. The rain fell like a sick affright
Of Nature at her work in killing him.
Memory of what he was gave no delight,
Delight at what he was was dead and dim.
O hands that once had clasped Hadrian's warm hands,
Whose cold now found them cold!
O hair bound erstwhile with the pressing bands!
O eyes half-diffidently bold!
O bare female male-body such
As a god's likeness to humanity!
O lips whose opening redness erst could touch
Lust's seats with a live art's variety!
O fingers skilled in things not to be told!
O tongue which, counter-tongued, made the blood bold!
O complete regency of lust throned on
Raged consciousness's spilled suspension!

171

These things are things that now must be no more.
The rain is silent, and the Emperor
Sinks by the couch. His grief is like a rage,
For the gods take away the life they give
And spoil the beauty they made live.
He weeps and knows that every future age
Is looking on him out of the to-be;
His love is on a universal stage;
A thousand unborn eyes weep with his misery.
Antinous is dead, is dead for ever,
Is dead for ever and all loves lament.
Venus herself, that was Adonis' lover,
Seeing him, that newly lived, now dead again,
Lends her old grief's renewal to be blent
With Hadrian's pain.
Now is Apollo sad because the stealer
Of his white body is for ever cold.
No careful kisses on that nippled point
Covering his heart-beats' silent place restore
His life again to ope his eyes and feel her
Presence along his veins Love's fortress hold.
No warmth of his another's warmth demands.
Now will his hands behind his head no more
Linked, in that posture giving all but hands,
On the projected body hands implore.
The rain falls, and he lies like one who hath
Forgotten all the gestures of his love
And lies awake waiting their hot return.
But all his arts and toys are now with Death.
This human ice no way of heat can move;
These ashes of a fire no flame can burn.
O Hadrian, what will now thy cold life be?
What boots it to be lord of men and might?
His absence o'er thy visible empery
Comes like a night,
Nor is there morn in hopes of new delight.
Now are thy nights widowed of love and kisses;
Now are thy days robbed of the night's awaiting;
Now have thy lips no purpose for thy blisses,
Left but to speak the name that Death is mating
With solitude and sorrow and affright.

Thy vague hands grope, as if they had dropped joy.
To hear that the rain ceases lift thy head,
And thy raised glance take to the lovely boy.
Naked he lies upon that memoried bed;
By thine own hand he lies uncoverèd.
There was he wont thy dangling sense to cloy,
And uncloy with more cloying, and annoy
With newer uncloying till thy senses bled.
His hand and mouth knew games to reinstall
Desire that thy worn spine was hurt to follow.
Sometimes it seemed to thee that all was hollow
In sense in each new straining of sucked lust.
Then still new turns of toying would he call
To thy nerves' flesh, and thou wouldst tremble and fall
Back on thy cushions with thy mind's sense hushed.

»Beautiful was my love, yet melancholy.
He had that art, that makes love captive wholly,
Of being slowly sad among lust's rages.
Now the Nile gave him up, the eternal Nile.
Under his wet locks Death's blue paleness wages
Now war upon our wishing with sad smile.«
Even as he thinks, the lust that is no more
Than a memory of lust revives and takes
His senses by the hand, his felt flesh wakes,
And all becomes again what 'twas before.
The dead body on the bed starts up and lives
And comes to lie with him, close, closer, and
A creeping love-wise and invisible hand
At every body-entrance to his lust
Whispers caresses which flit off yet just
Remain enough to bleed his last nerve's strand,
O sweet and cruel Parthian fugitives!
So he half rises, looking on his lover,
That now can love nothing but what none know.
Vaguely, half-seeing what he doth behold,
He runs his cold lips all the body over.
And so ice-senseless are his lips that, lo!,
He scarce tastes death from the dead body's cold,
But it seems both are dead or living both
And love is still the presence and the mover.

Then his lips cease on the other lips' cold sloth.
Ah, there the wanting breath reminds his lips
That from beyond the gods hath moved a mist
Between him and this boy. His finger-tips,
Still idly searching o'er the body, list
For some flesh-response to their waking mood.
But their love-question is not understood:
The god is dead whose cult was to be kissed!
He lifts his hand up to where heaven should be
And cries on the mute gods to know bis pain.
Let your calm faces turn aside to his plea,
O granting powers! He will yield up his reign.
In the still deserts he will parchèd live,
In the far barbarous roads beggar or slave,
But to his arms again the warm boy give!
Forego that space ye meant to be his grave!
Take all the female loveliness of earth
And in one mound of death its remnant spill!
But, by sweet Ganymede, that Jove found worth
And above Hebe did elect to fill
His cup at his high feasting, and instil
The friendlier love that fills the other's dearth,
The clod of female embraces resolve
To dust, o father of the gods, but spare
This boy and his white body and golden hair!
Maybe thy better Ganymede thou feel'st
That he should be, and out of jealous care
From Hadrian's arms to thine his beauty steal'st.
He was a kitten playing with lust, playing
With his own and with Hadrian's, sometimes one
And sometimes two, now linking, now undone;
Now leaving lust, now lust's high lusts delaying;
Now eying lust not wide, but from askance
Jumping round on lust's half-unexpectance;
Now softly gripping, then with fury holding,
Now playfully playing, now seriously, now lying
By th' side of lust looking at it, now spying
Which way to take lust in his lust's withholding.
Thus did the hours slide from their tangled hands
And from their mixèd limbs the moments slip.
Now were his arms dead leaves, now iron bands;

Now were his lips cups, now the things that sip;
Now were his eyes too closed and now too looking;
Now were his uncontinuings frenzy working;
Now were his arts a feather and now a whip.
That love they lived as a religion
Offered to gods that come themselves to men.
Sometimes he was adorned or made to don
Half-vestures, then in statued nudity
Did imitate some god that seems to be
By marble's accurate virtue men's again.
Now was he Venus, white out of the seas;
And now was he Apollo, young and golden;
Now as Jove sate he in mock judgement over
The presence at his feet of his slaved lover;
Now was he an acted rite, by one beholden,
In ever-repositioned mysteries.
Now he is something anyone can be.
O stark negation of the thing it is!
O golden-haired moon-cold loveliness!
Too cold! too cold! and love as cold as he!
Love through the memories of his love doth roam
As through a labyrinth, in sad madness glad,
And now calls on his name and bids him come,
And now is smiling at his imaged coming
That is i'th' heart like faces in the gloaming –
Mere shining shadows of the forms they had.
The rain again like a vague pain arose
And put the sense of wetness in the air.
Suddenly did the Emperor suppose
He saw this room and all in it from far.
He saw the couch, the boy, and his own frame
Cast down against the couch, and he became
A clearer presence to himself, and said
These words unuttered, save to his soul's dread:

»I shall build thee a statue that will be
To the continued future evidence
Of my love and thy beauty and the sense
That beauty giveth of divinity.
Though death with subtle uncovering hands remove
The apparel of life and empire from our love,

Yet its nude statue, that thou dost inspirit,
All future times, whether they will't or not,
Shall, like a gift a forcing god hath brought,
Inevitably inherit.

»Ay, this thy statue shall I build, and set
Upon the pinnacle of being thine, that Time
By its subtle dim crime
Will fear to eat it from life, or to fret
With war's or envy's rage from bulk and stone.
Fate cannot be that! Gods themselves, that make
Things change, Fate's own hand, that doth overtake
The gods themselves with darkness, will draw back
From marring thus thy statue and my boon,
Leaving the wide world hollow with thy lack.

»This picture of our love will bridge the ages.
It will loom white out of the past and be
Eternal, like a Roman victory,
In every heart the future will give rages
Of not being our love's contemporary.

»Yet oh that this were needed not, and thou
Wert the red flower perfuming my life,
The garland on the brows of my delight,
The living flame on altars of my soul!
Would all this were a thing thou mightest now
Smile at from under thy death-mocking lids
And wonder that I should so put a strife
Twixt me and gods for thy lost presence bright;
Were there nought in this but my empty dole
And thy awakening smile half to condole
With what my dreaming pain to hope forbids.«
Thus went he, like a lover who is waiting,
From place to place in this dim doubting mind.
Now was his hope a great intention fating
Its wish to being, now felt he he was blind
In some point of his seen wish undefined.
When love meets death we know not what to feel.
When death foils love we know not what to know.
Now did his doubt hope, now did his hope doubt;

Now what his wish dreamed the dream's sense did flout
And to a sullen emptiness congeal.
Then again the gods fanned love's darkening glow.

»Thy death has given me a higher lust –
A flash-lust raging for eternity.
On mine imperial fate I set my trust
That the high gods, that made me emperor be,
Will not annul from a more real life
My wish that thou should'st live for e'er and stand
A fleshly presence on their better land,
More lovely yet not lovelier, for there
No things impossible our wishes mar
Nor pain our hearts with change and time and strife.

»Love, love, my love! thou art already a god.
This thought of mine, which I a wish believe,
Is no wish, but a sight, to me allowed
By the great gods, that love love and can give
To mortal hearts, under the shape of wishes –
Of wishes having undiscovered reaches –,
A vision of the real things beyond
Our life-imprisoned life, our sense-bound sense.
Ay, what I wish thee to be thou art now
Already. Already on Olympic ground
Thou walkest and art perfect, yet art thou,
For thou needst no excess of thee to don
Perfect to be, being perfection.

»My heart is singing like a morning bird.
A great hope from the gods comes down to me
And bids my heart to subtler sense be stirred
And think not that strange evil of thee
That to think thee mortal would be.

»My love, my love, my god-love! Let me kiss
On thy cold lips thy hot lips now immortal,
Greeting thee at Death's portal's happiness,
For to the gods Death's portal is Life's portal.

»Were no Olympus yet for thee, my love

Would make thee one, where thou sole god mightst prove,
And I thy sole adorer, glad to be
Thy sole adorer through infinity.
That were a universe divine enough
For love and me and what to me thou art.
To have thee is a thing made of gods' stuff
And to look on thee eternity's best part.

»But this is true and mine own art: the god
Thou art now is a body made by me,
For, if thou art now flesh reality
Beyond where men age and night cometh still,
'Tis to my love's great making power thou owest
That life thou on thy memory bestowest
And mak'st it carnal. Had my love not held
An empire of my mighty legioned will,
Thou to gods' consort hadst not been compelled.

»My love that found thee, when it found thee did
But find its own true body and exact look.
Therefore when now thy memory I bid
Become a god where gods are, I but move
To death's high column's top the shape it took
And set it there for vision of all love.

»O love, my love, put up with my strong will
Of loving to Olympus, be thou there
The latest god whose honey-coloured hair
Takes divine eyes! As thou wert on earth, still
In heaven bodyfully be and roam,
A prisoner of that happiness of home,
With elder gods, while I on earth do make
A statue for thy deathlessness' seen sake.

»Yet thy true deadless statue I shall build
Will be no stone thing, but that same regret
By which our love's eternity is willed.
One side of that is thou, as gods see thee
Now, and the other, here, thy memory.
My sorrow will make that men's god, and set
Thy naked memory on the parapet

That looks upon the seas of future times.
Some will say all our love was but our crimes;
Others against our names the knives will whet
Of their glad hate of beauty's beauty, and make
Our names a base of heap whereon to rake
The names of all our brothers with quick scorn.
Yet will our presence, like eternal Morn,
Ever return at Beauty's hour, and shine
Out of the East of Love, in light to enshrine
New gods to come, the lacking world to adorn.

»All that thou art now is thyself and I.
Our dual presence has its unity
In that perfection of body which my love,
By loving it, became, and did from life
Raise into godness, calm above the strife
Of times, and changing passions far above.

»But since men see more with the eyes than soul,
Still I in stone shall utter this great dole;
Still, eager that men hunger by thy presence,
I shall to marble carry this regret
That in my heart like a great star is set.
Thus, even in stone, our love shall stand so great
In thy statue of us, like a god's fate,
Our love's incarnate and discarnate essence,
That, like a trumpet reaching over seas
And going from continent to continent,
Our love shall speak its joy and woe, death-blent,
Over infinities and eternities.

»And here, memory or statue, we shall stand,
Still the same one, as we were hand in hand
Nor felt each other's hand for feeling feeling.
Men still will see me when thy sense they take.
The entire gods might pass in the vast wheeling
Of the globed ages. If but for thy sake,
That, being theirs, hadst gone with their gone band,
They would return, as they had slept to wake.

»Then the end of days when Jove were born again

And Ganymede again pour at his feast
Would see our dual soul from death released
And recreated unto joy, fear, pain –
All that love doth contain;
Life – all the beauty that doth make a lust
Of love's own true love, at the spell amazed;
And, if our very memory wore to dust,
By some gods' race of the end of ages must
Our dual unity again be raised.«

It rained still. But slow-treading night came in,

Closing the weary eyelids of each sense.

The very consciousness of self and soul

Grew, like a landscape through dim raining, dim.

The Emperor lay still, so still that now

He half forgot where now he lay, or whence

The sorrow that was still salt on his lips.

All had been something very far, a scroll

Rolled up. The things he felt were like the rim

That haloes round the moon when the night weeps.

His head was bowed into his arms, and they

On the low couch, foreign to his sense, lay.

His closed eyes seemed open to him, and seeing

The naked floor, dark, cold, sad and unmeaning.

His hurting breath was all his sense could know.

Out of the falling darkness the wind rose

And fell; a voice swooned in the courts below;

And the Emperor slept.

And the Emperor slept. The gods came now

And bore something away, no sense knows how,

On unseen arms of power and repose.

INDEX

A

A Martian Muse, 4, 122, 2
Aaron Copland, 38, 107
Aaron Shurin, 163
Aaron Smith, 140
Adam Kirsch, 82, 113, 114, 122, 124, 127, 128, 130, 167
Adolphus Hailstork, 12, 34
Adrienne Rich, 69
Albert Camus, 1, 9, 161
Alban Berg, 16, 110, 111
Alex Ross, i, ii, 105, 106, 107, 108, 109
Alfred Corn, 137
Allen Grossman, 58
Alvin Feinman, 163
American in Paris, 11, 110, 111
American Poetry Review, 125
André Gide, 1, 4, 5, 6, 9, 125
Andrew Ross, 158
Andrew Sullivan, 146
Angel, Interrupted, 4, 2
Ann Lauterbach, i, ii, 62, 73, 76, 115, 122
Anthropos, 30
Antinous, 1, ii, 19, 26, 171, 172, 2
Antonio Skarmeta, 10
Aqualung, 3, 40, 96, 97, 98
Arnold Whittall, 129
Arthur Ransome, 146
Arthur Upfield, 146
Arvo Pärt, 34
Atlanta Symphony, 13, 14, 29, 31
Austin Tappan Wright, 146

B

Basho, 20
black, iii, iv, 2, 11, 13, 53, 54, 64, 74, 84, 142, 163
Bob Dylan, 38, 95
Bournemouth Symphony, 34
Bow Down in Jericho, 18
Brad Richard, 142, 148
Brenda Hillman, 157
Brian Teare, 139
Byron Herbert Reece, 18, 24, 26

C

C.E.S. Wood, 9

Cameron La Follette, 2, 146
Camille Paglia, 9, 68
cancer, 1, 3, 88, 93, 94, 98, 99, 101, 102, 103, 104, 105, 109, 128, 155
Carl Morse, 138
Carl Phillips, 2, 11, 13, 18, 74, 75, 76, 141, 146
Carmina Burana, 29, 31
Ce Rosenow, 146
Charles Bernstein, 131
Charles Simic, 113, 114, 146
Chris Cutrone, 85
Christian Wiman, 103, 104, 122, 126
Christopher Hennessy, 120, 134
Chuck Marx, 152
Claude Lévi-Strauss, 30
Colin Brumby, 33, 41, 68, 73, 96, 107
Columbia University, 3, 98, 128
Constantine Cavafy, 20
Cornell University, 2, 37
Czeslaw Milosz, 5

D

D. A. Powell, 163
Dan Simmons, 143
Dana Gioia, 72
David Alan Miller, 106
"David and Jonathan," 18, 26
David Laing, 20
David Trinidad, 135
David Wojahn, 13
David Yezzi, 72
Divisi, 37, 38, 39
Donald Britton, 163
Drew Lanham, 53
Duchamp, 17
"Dumbarton Oaks" concerto, 15
Dusty Springfield, 152

E

Edmund Wilson, 68
Edna St. Vincent Millay, 56
Edward Elgar, 68
Edward Hirsch, 26
Edwin Muir, 68, 148, 149
Elizabeth Bishop, 125
Elizabeth Hand, 143
Elizabeth Smart, 42
Elliott Coues, 4
Emily Dickinson, 20, 128
emo, 3, 97, 98
Essex Hemphill, 74

Evan Eisenberg, 77, 79
"Eve's Awakening," 11
Evergreen State College, 24
Ezra Pound, 129, 152

F

Fall Out Boy, 3, 98
Fata Morgana, 4, 11, 12, 58, 2
Federico Garcia Lorca, 6
Fireweed, 23
Frances Hodgson Burnett, 146
Frank Bidart, 136

G

Gabriela Mistral, 18
Garrick Ohlsson, 15
Gary Snyder, 20
gay, iii, iv, 2, 8, 19, 35, 74, 84, 91, 120, 132, 134, 141, 142, 148, 149, 163, 167;
    homosexual, 35, 138, 143, 159
George Barker, i, ii, 42
George Gollin, 68
Gertrude Stein, 63
Gore Vidal, 9, 35, 145, 146
Gwyneth Jones, 143

H

Hannah Wilson, 20, 22
Hans Lodeizen, 82
Heidi Schellman, 68
HIV, 24, 101, 104

I

Inside Higher Education, ii, 11, 13
Ira Gershwin, 11, 18, 110
Isaac Asimov, 146

J

Jackson Pollock, 17
Jay Parini, 162
J. D. McClatchy, 2, 7, 9, 18, 61, 138, 141, 159
James Merrill, 7, 18, 35, 61, 81, 106, 113, 114, 125, 148, 152, 159
Jean Genet, 163
Joan Larkin, 136
Joanna Russ, 143
John Ashbery, 157, 158, 160
John Jay Chapman, 6, 9, 52, 65, 66, 68, 146, 2
John Tavener, 34

Jonathan Livingston Seagull, 11, 12
Jorie Graham, 85, 158, 163
Jose Serebrier, 34
Joshua Clover, 149, 150
James Joyce, 158

K

Karen Ford, 73, 74, 93, 112, 131, 157, 158, 169
Kate Bush, 118, 119, 120, 130
Kevin Young, 24
Khaled Hosseini, 145

L

L. E. Sissman, 104
Lawrence Rainey, 129
Lee Hoiby, 34
Leonard Cirino, 146
Leonard Cohen, 37
Linda Gregg, 163
Loren Eiseley, 20, 68

M

Malheur Field Station, 162, 166
Mark Doty, 136, 141
Mei-mei Berssenbrugge, 56
Michael Anania, 59
Michael Oakeshott, 9
Michael Retter, 19
Michael Spring, 20, 21, 22
Michel de Montaigne, 9
Moby Dick, 145
Mozart, piano concerto no. 17, 15

N

"Narcissus to Echo," 11
Nathan Myers, 106
nature, 7, 8, 20, 38, 48, 54, 64, 91, 123, 124, 136, 163
Ned Rorem, i, ii, 7, 33, 36, 38, 112
Noam Chomsky, 67, 70

O

On the Rocks, 36, 95
Oregon, ii, 1, 10, 20, 22, 26, 27, 37, 41, 53, 67, 69, 89, 101, 102, 108, 114, 154, 156, 160, 161, 162, 168, 2
Orpheus in the Bronx, i, ii, 3, 4, 98, 99, 100, 101, 115, 122, 153, 156, 158, 159, 161, 163, 165, 168, 2
Otherhood, 4, 2

P

Pablo Neruda, 10, 18, 24, 26
Patrick O'Brian, 2, 120, 146, 160
Pattiann Rogers, 19, 20, 124
Paul Valéry, 5, 6, 9, 69
Pensacola Opera, 13
Fernando Pessoa, 1, ii, 18, 19, 26, 171, 2
Phil Ochs, 5, 26, 96, 97
Robert Philen, 1, ii, v, 4, 7, 11, 14, 17, 29, 39, 2
Pablo Picasso, 17
post-avant, 131, 152

R

Rafael Campo, 140
Ralph Waldo Emerson, 9
Ray Bradbury, 146
Red Clay Weather, 4, 2
Rich Hoyer, 19, 119
Richard Dawkins, 70
Richard Lederer, 102
Rick Barot, 139
Robert Duncan, 43, 152
Robert Lax, 5
Robert McDowell, 159
Robert Spano, 14, 31
Roland Greene, 131
Ron Silliman, 77
Rula Lenska, 68

S

Samuel Barber, 24, 68
Samuel R. Delany, 2, 143, 155, 156, 157, 163, 165, 166
Satyricon, 147
Schoenberg, 16, 106, 107, 110, 111
Shaun Davey, 33, 96
Simon Rattle, 31
Some are Drowning, 4, 2
Sonata da Chiesa, 12, 34
Stephen Spender, 125, 148, 149, 157
Stephen Maturin, 2
Stravinsky, i, ii, 14, 15, 17, 29, 31, 107, 110

T

T. S. Eliot, 43, 158
The Chronicle of Higher Education, 71
The Raw and the Cooked, 30
The Rite of Spring, i, ii, 13, 14, 15, 17, 29, 31
Theodor Adorno, iv, 85, 143, 144

Theodore Roethke, 3
Thomas M. Disch, 157
Thomas Merton, 5
Thomas Wentworth Higginson, 128
Tim Dlugos, 163
"Turandot," 11, 13
Ture Rangstrom, 34, 96

U

University of Iowa, 2
University of Oregon, 1, 7, 18, 36, 39, 69, 87, 95, 141, 2
Ursula K. Le Guin, 132, 156

V

Vernon Shetley, 66, 80
Virgil Thomson, 68

W

Wallace Stevens, 87, 88, 153, 154, 163
W. H. Auden, 18, 42, 57, 125, 146
W. S. Merwin, 2, 20, 69, 71, 72, 146
Wendell Berry, 20, 68
"While the Temptations," 11
William Carlos Williams, 56
William Hawley, 34
Wrong, 2, 4,

Y

Yusef Komunyakaa, 11, 13, 24

The late **Reginald Shepherd** was one of the nation's finest poets. A graduate of the University of Iowa and Brown University, his works include *Some are Drowning* (1994); *Angel, Interrupted* (1996); *Wrong* (1999); *Otherhood* (2003); *Fata Morgana* (2007); *Orpheus in the Bronx* (2007, Michigan), *A Martian Muse* (2010, Michigan) and *Red Clay Weather* (2011); all from Pittsburgh except as noted.

Alan Contreras is a semi-retired education official. A graduate of the University of Oregon and its law school, he served as co-editor of *Birds of Oregon* (Oregon State University Press, 2003) and has published other natural history titles. OSU Press also published his memoir *Afield* (2009). His recent books include *College and State* (2013) and *An Introduction to John Jay Chapman's Philosophy of Higher Education* (2013). He has also published poetry and reviews in several venues. He blogs at *The Oregon Review* (oregonreview.blogspot.com) and lives in Oregon.

Robert Philen is Associate Professor of Anthropology at the University of Western Florida and literary executor for Reginald Shepherd, his late partner. He is an avid birder, an ardent fan of poetry, music, and painting, an anthropologist of many topics, and editor of Shepherd's posthumous collections *A Martian Muse* and *Red Clay Weather*. He blogs at *Robert Philen's Blog* (robertphilen.blogspot.com).

Fernando Pessoa was a Portuguese poet who sometimes wrote in English. His long poem *Antinous* has rarely been published. It was written in English in 1918.

www.ingramcontent.com/pod-product-compliance
Lightning Source LLC
Chambersburg PA
CBHW030334030726
47499CB00003B/763